ARTIFICIAL INTELLIGENCE FOR PHARMACEUTICAL FIELD FORCE EFFECTIVENESS

A Practical Framework for Commercial Leadership, Sales Excellence, and Organizational Transformation

TEVFIK TOLGA KAVUN

Staten House
Orlando | 2026

FOREWORD

Artificial Intelligence Will Not Replace Great Leaders

Throughout history, every major technological breakthrough has raised the same question.

"Will technology replace people?"

The emergence of Artificial Intelligence has generated similar discussions across nearly every industry, including pharmaceutical commercial organizations.

Many executives understandably ask whether AI will eventually replace Medical Representatives, Regional Managers, or even commercial leadership itself.

In my opinion, this question reflects a misunderstanding of what Artificial Intelligence is truly designed to accomplish.

Artificial Intelligence is not a replacement for leadership.

It is a multiplier of leadership.

Technology can analyze millions of data points within seconds.

It can identify patterns invisible to human observation.

It can forecast future trends with remarkable accuracy.

However, Artificial Intelligence cannot inspire people.

It cannot build trust.

It cannot coach struggling employees.

It cannot navigate organizational politics.

It cannot understand culture.

Most importantly, it cannot lead.

Leadership remains profoundly human.

During more than two decades of managing pharmaceutical commercial organizations, I have learned that sustainable business success has never depended solely upon products, technology, or organizational size.

It has depended upon the quality of leadership.

Organizations rarely fail because they lack information.

They fail because they make poor decisions.

Artificial Intelligence offers something fundamentally different.

It provides leaders with better information, better forecasts, and better analytical capabilities.

Yet every meaningful decision still requires human judgment, professional experience, ethical responsibility, and organizational wisdom.

This book is therefore not about Artificial Intelligence itself.

It is about better leadership.

Artificial Intelligence simply provides a new generation of leaders with capabilities that previous generations could only imagine.

Those organizations capable of combining experienced leadership with intelligent decision-support systems will define the future of pharmaceutical commercial excellence.

The purpose of this book is not to predict the future.

Its purpose is to help commercial leaders build it.

Tevfik Tolga Kavun

BOOK EDITION

Artificial Intelligence for Pharmaceutical Field Force Effectiveness
A Practical Framework for Commercial Leadership, Sales Excellence, and Organizational Transformation

Tevfik Tolga Kavun
ORCID: https://orcid.org/0009-0000-2073-0201
Original publication DOI: https://doi.org/10.5281/zenodo.21853513

First Edition | 2026

Staten House
Orlando, Florida, USA
Paperback ISBN: 979-8-90678-571-8
www.tevfiktolgakavun.com

This book substantially expands, reorganizes, and applies ideas first introduced in the author's original research publication cited above. The underlying frameworks and interpretations are the author's original practitioner contributions.

Professional disclaimer: This book is intended for leadership education and strategic discussion. It does not provide medical, legal, regulatory, compliance, or investment advice. Illustrative scenarios are composites and do not disclose confidential company information.

About This Book

This book examines how Artificial Intelligence is reshaping pharmaceutical commercial leadership, arguing that AI strengthens leadership by extending managerial judgment, pattern recognition, and decision support; it is not a substitute for the leader. Drawing on more than two decades of the author's experience managing multinational pharmaceutical field organizations, together with established leadership and management literature, the book traces the historical evolution of pharmaceutical commercial organizations through four eras and proposes two original conceptual models: the Kavun Adaptive Commercial Leadership Framework™ (KACL) and the Field Force Operating System™ (FFOS). These models describe how human leadership, organizational intelligence, and Artificial Intelligence can be integrated to support predictive decision-making, adaptive territory management, AI-assisted leadership coaching, and continuous organizational learning within pharmaceutical commercial operations. The book further discusses practical implementation phases, common transformation failures, and the anticipated evolution of Medical Representative, Regional Manager, and Field Force Manager roles toward 2035. As a conceptual and practitioner-oriented contribution rather than an empirical study, the book concludes by acknowledging its limitations and proposing directions for future empirical and interdisciplinary research on AI-augmented commercial leadership in the pharmaceutical industry.

Keywords: Artificial Intelligence; pharmaceutical commercial leadership; predictive management; organizational learning; territory management; leadership coaching; decision intelligence.

Introduction: Scope and Approach

This book is a conceptual and practitioner-oriented book. It does not report original experimental, clinical, or statistical research. The analysis synthesizes established literature in management, organizational learning, Artificial Intelligence, AI governance, and pharmaceutical commercial operations with the author's professional experience leading multinational pharmaceutical field organizations.

Industry and professional sources are used to contextualize current developments in AI-enabled commercial leadership. The Kavun Adaptive Commercial Leadership Framework™ (KACL) and the Field Force Operating System™ (FFOS) are proposed as original conceptual models intended for practitioner application, scholarly discussion, and future empirical evaluation. Illustrative scenarios in this book are explanatory and should not be read as results of controlled studies. The Limitations and Future Research sections therefore identify where empirical validation and further interdisciplinary research are required.

TABLE OF CONTENTS

1.1 Introduction

Every pharmaceutical executive faces the same strategic challenge:

How can a commercial organization continue to grow while market access becomes more difficult, healthcare professionals become less accessible, compliance requirements increase, and organizational costs continue to rise?

For more than seventy years, pharmaceutical companies have relied on field-based commercial organizations as the primary channel for communicating scientific information, building professional relationships, and supporting the appropriate use of medicines. Throughout this period, the pharmaceutical field force evolved from a product-centered sales organization into a sophisticated commercial ecosystem integrating medical education, customer engagement, market intelligence, data analytics, and cross-functional collaboration (World Health Organization, 2021; IQVIA, 2024).

Yet despite extraordinary scientific advances, the management philosophy governing most pharmaceutical sales organizations has changed far more slowly than the environment in which those organizations operate.

Traditional management models continue to emphasize historical sales performance, managerial intuition, periodic performance reviews, and static territory structures. While these methods have supported decades of commercial success, they were developed during an era in which market conditions changed relatively slowly, customer expectations remained predictable, and commercial data were limited (Drucker, 2007; Mintzberg, 1973).

Today's commercial environment is fundamentally different from the one in which traditional pharmaceutical management practices were originally developed.

Healthcare systems are becoming increasingly data-driven. Physicians interact with pharmaceutical companies through multiple digital and face-to-face channels. Regulatory expectations continue to expand. Product portfolios have become increasingly specialized, while competition has intensified across nearly every therapeutic area (Deloitte, 2025; IQVIA, 2024).

At the same time, commercial leaders are expected to make faster decisions based upon substantially larger volumes of information than ever before (McKinsey & Company, 2025a).

This transformation has fundamentally changed the role of commercial leadership.

Commercial leadership is no longer defined solely by achieving sales targets. Increasingly, it is defined by the ability to transform growing volumes of information into timely, high-quality organizational decisions. This shift provides the foundation for the leadership model proposed throughout this book.

Success no longer depends primarily upon increasing the number of Medical Representatives.

Instead, sustainable competitive advantage increasingly depends upon how effectively organizations transform information into decisions.

Artificial Intelligence represents perhaps the most important technological development capable of supporting this transformation (Russell & Norvig, 2021).

However, contrary to many popular discussions surrounding AI, its greatest value within pharmaceutical commercial organizations is unlikely to come from replacing human decision-makers.

Its greatest value lies in augmenting managerial judgment.

AI can help experienced commercial leaders make better decisions by identifying patterns, forecasting outcomes, evaluating alternative scenarios, and continuously learning from organizational data.

For Field Force Managers, Regional Managers, Commercial Directors, and executive leadership teams, this represents a significant shift in managerial capability.

Instead of relying primarily upon historical reports and subjective interpretation, leaders can increasingly utilize predictive intelligence to guide organizational strategy, workforce planning, coaching priorities, territory optimization, customer engagement strategies, and commercial resource allocation.

This evolution represents far more than technological modernization.

It reflects a fundamental shift in how commercial organizations create competitive advantage. In previous decades, success depended largely upon expanding field force capacity and improving execution. Today, sustainable advantage increasingly depends upon how effectively leaders convert information into organizational intelligence and organizational intelligence into consistently better decisions.

It represents the beginning of a new management philosophy.

Throughout this book, Artificial Intelligence is therefore examined not as an isolated technological innovation but as an organizational capability capable of reshaping how pharmaceutical companies plan, manage, develop, and continuously improve commercial field organizations.

1.2 From Product Selling to Commercial Leadership

The history of pharmaceutical field organizations closely mirrors the evolution of the pharmaceutical industry itself (Porter, 1985; Drucker, 2007).

During much of the twentieth century, commercial success depended largely on expanding sales coverage. Companies increased the number of Medical Representatives, expanded geographic territories, and relied heavily on personal relationships with physicians. Performance was primarily evaluated through prescription volume, sales growth, and market share (Zoltners et al., 2009).

As healthcare systems matured, however, the role of the Medical Representative gradually evolved.

Scientific discussions became more complex.

Healthcare professionals expected evidence-based conversations rather than promotional presentations.

Product differentiation became increasingly dependent upon clinical outcomes, health economics, and patient value (Porter & Teisberg, 2006; IQVIA, 2024).

Consequently, commercial leadership also evolved.

The responsibilities of Field Force Managers expanded well beyond supervising sales activities.

Modern pharmaceutical leaders became responsible for organizational development, talent management, leadership coaching, commercial planning, cross-functional collaboration, compliance oversight, customer engagement strategy, and continuous performance improvement (Mintzberg, 1973; Kotter, 2012).

Today, effective commercial leadership requires balancing scientific credibility, commercial execution, regulatory compliance, digital transformation, workforce development, and financial discipline simultaneously (Senge, 2006; Heifetz et al., 2009).

This evolution illustrates a broader shift in leadership theory. Modern pharmaceutical leaders are no longer evaluated solely by operational execution, but by their ability to integrate scientific expertise, organizational capability, digital technologies, and strategic decision-making into a coherent commercial system. Leadership has therefore evolved from operational supervision toward organizational orchestration.

This growing complexity explains why traditional management approaches are becoming increasingly insufficient.

Organizations no longer require managers who merely supervise sales teams.

They require leaders capable of integrating people, processes, technology, and data into a unified commercial strategy.

Artificial Intelligence provides an unprecedented opportunity to support this transition.

Yet technology alone cannot create commercial excellence.

Only organizations that combine experienced leadership with intelligent decision-support systems will achieve sustainable competitive advantage in the coming decade (Brynjolfsson & McAfee, 2014; McKinsey & Company, 2025a).

1.3 The Four Historical Eras of Pharmaceutical Commercial Organizations

The commercial organization has remained the cornerstone of pharmaceutical market engagement for more than half a century. However, its responsibilities, operating model, and success factors have evolved significantly in response to scientific innovation, healthcare reforms, technological advancements, and changing expectations from healthcare professionals.

Understanding this evolution is essential for appreciating why Artificial Intelligence should not be viewed merely as another digital tool, but rather as the next major transformation in commercial leadership.

The evolution of pharmaceutical commercial organizations can be broadly divided into four distinct eras.

Era I: Product-Centered Selling (1950–1990)

For several decades, pharmaceutical companies operated in an environment characterized by limited competition, relatively stable healthcare systems, and fewer regulatory constraints.

During this period, Medical Representatives primarily served as product promoters. Their principal objective was to increase product awareness among physicians through regular face-to-face visits. Commercial success depended largely on:

- Expanding sales force size
- Increasing physician coverage
- Product knowledge
- Personal relationships
- Sales call frequency

Field managers primarily supervised activity levels rather than organizational performance. Leadership focused on monitoring field visits, coaching product presentations, and achieving monthly sales targets.

Commercial decision-making relied heavily on managerial experience rather than systematic data analysis.

Although highly effective for its time, this model assumed that greater promotional activity would naturally generate greater commercial success (Zoltners et al., 2009).

Era II: Customer-Centric Commercial Excellence (1990–2010)

Healthcare systems became increasingly sophisticated during the 1990s. Scientific evidence gained greater importance, healthcare professionals became more specialized, and governments introduced stricter reimbursement and regulatory requirements.

As a result, pharmaceutical companies shifted from product promotion toward customer-centric commercial excellence.

Medical Representatives gradually evolved from sales representatives into scientific communicators capable of discussing clinical evidence, treatment guidelines, patient outcomes, and comparative therapeutic value (Porter & Teisberg, 2006; IQVIA, 2024).

Commercial organizations also became significantly more complex.

Field Force Managers were no longer responsible solely for supervising representatives (Mintzberg, 1973; Kotter, 2012).

Their responsibilities expanded to include:

- Territory optimization
- Workforce planning
- Regional resource allocation
- Leadership coaching
- Performance management
- Customer segmentation
- Commercial planning

This period also witnessed the emergence of Customer Relationship Management (CRM) systems, enabling companies to collect and organize significantly larger volumes of commercial information than ever before.

However, despite improved access to information, managerial decisions remained predominantly human-driven.

This period marked an important transition in pharmaceutical leadership. Competitive advantage no longer depended solely on expanding sales activity, but increasingly on developing organizational capabilities that could sustain scientific engagement, customer relationships, and cross-functional collaboration.

Era III: Digital Commercial Transformation (2010–2025)

The rapid expansion of digital technologies fundamentally altered how pharmaceutical companies interacted with healthcare professionals.

Physicians increasingly expected multichannel engagement instead of relying exclusively on traditional face-to-face visits.

Commercial organizations therefore integrated multiple communication channels, including:

- Remote detailing
- Video conferencing
- Digital education platforms
- Marketing automation
- Customer portals
- Omnichannel communication strategies

Business Intelligence platforms became standard components of commercial organizations.

Large volumes of commercial information—including CRM activity, prescription trends, market access data, physician segmentation, customer engagement metrics, and operational KPIs—became readily available to managers.

Ironically, however, the abundance of information created a new challenge.

Managers now possessed more data than they could reasonably interpret.

Decision-making became increasingly complex.

Traditional reporting systems generated descriptive information, but rarely provided predictive recommendations.

Commercial leaders still needed to determine:

- Which physician should receive additional attention?
- Which territory required restructuring?
- Which Regional Manager needed coaching?
- Which representative presented the highest development potential?

These decisions continued to rely heavily upon managerial judgment.

Era IV: AI-Augmented Commercial Leadership (2025–Future)

Artificial Intelligence represents the beginning of a fundamentally different management paradigm.

Unlike previous technological innovations that primarily improved efficiency, AI directly enhances managerial decision-making.

Instead of simply reporting historical performance, AI can identify hidden commercial patterns, forecast future outcomes, recommend corrective actions, and continuously improve its recommendations as new organizational data become available.

Within pharmaceutical commercial organizations, AI has the potential to support virtually every managerial function, including:

- Sales forecasting
- Territory optimization
- Workforce planning
- Coaching prioritization
- Leadership development
- Customer segmentation
- Resource allocation
- Predictive performance management
- Omnichannel engagement planning
- Commercial risk identification

Importantly, AI should not be viewed as a replacement for experienced commercial leaders.

Instead, it functions as a decision-support capability that amplifies managerial expertise while reducing uncertainty associated with increasingly complex commercial environments.

Organizations capable of integrating experienced leadership with advanced analytical technologies will likely outperform competitors that continue relying exclusively on traditional management models.

Figure 1

Evolution of Pharmaceutical Commercial Organizations

Era	Primary Focus	Leadership Style	Technology
1950–1990	Product Promotion	Activity Management	Paper-Based

Era	Primary Focus	Leadership Style	Technology
1990–2010	Customer-Centric Sales	Performance Management	CRM Systems
2010–2025	Digital Transformation	Data-Driven Leadership	Business Intelligence
2025+	AI-Augmented Commercial Leadership	Predictive Leadership	Artificial Intelligence

Interpretation of Figure 1

The four historical eras presented above illustrate that pharmaceutical commercial organizations have consistently evolved in response to changes in science, healthcare systems, customer expectations, and technology.

Each transition expanded not only the responsibilities of Medical Representatives but also the strategic role of commercial leadership.

Artificial Intelligence therefore represents the continuation of this historical evolution rather than a disruption of it.

The central argument of this book is that the next competitive advantage will emerge not from technology alone, but from leaders capable of integrating human judgment with predictive intelligence.

Importantly, this progression should not be interpreted as the replacement of one management philosophy by another. Instead, each evolutionary stage builds upon the capabilities of the previous one, with Artificial Intelligence extending—not replacing—the strategic role of commercial leadership.

Chapter Key Takeaways

- Pharmaceutical commercial organizations have evolved from activity-based sales organizations into complex, data-driven leadership structures.
- The responsibilities of Field Force Managers have expanded significantly over the past three decades.
- Digital transformation increased data availability but also increased managerial complexity.
- Artificial Intelligence should be viewed as a leadership enabler rather than a replacement for human expertise.
- The next competitive advantage will come from combining experienced leadership with predictive intelligence.

Author's Insight

During more than two decades of leadership in multinational pharmaceutical organizations, I observed that the most successful field organizations were not necessarily those with the largest sales forces. They were the organizations that consistently transformed commercial information into better managerial decisions. Artificial Intelligence has the potential to accelerate this transformation—but only when combined with experienced leadership, disciplined execution, and a culture of continuous learning.

1.4 Why Traditional Management Is Reaching Its Limits

For decades, pharmaceutical commercial organizations have relied upon managerial experience, standardized reporting systems, and historical sales performance as the primary foundations for commercial decision-making. These practices have produced considerable business success and remain valuable components of effective commercial leadership. However, the business environment in which pharmaceutical organizations now operate has changed fundamentally.

Modern commercial organizations generate extraordinary volumes of information every day. Customer Relationship Management (CRM) systems capture thousands of physician interactions. Business Intelligence platforms continuously update sales performance indicators. Digital engagement platforms measure physician behavior across multiple communication channels. Marketing automation systems produce campaign analytics in real time, while enterprise resource planning systems provide continuous operational and financial visibility (Davenport & Harris, 2007; Gartner, 2024a).

Paradoxically, the challenge facing commercial leaders today is no longer the absence of information but the inability to transform information into timely, actionable managerial decisions.

Field Force Managers frequently receive dozens of reports every week covering sales performance, call activity, territory coverage, physician segmentation, market share, product mix, customer engagement, training completion, compliance indicators, incentive compensation, and employee performance. While each report offers valuable information independently, very few explain what actions managers should actually take.

Consequently, many important commercial decisions continue to depend largely upon managerial intuition rather than systematic predictive analysis (Kahneman, 2011).

For example, managers routinely ask questions such as:

- Which Regional Manager requires immediate coaching?
- Which Medical Representative demonstrates the highest future leadership potential?
- Which territory should be restructured before commercial performance begins to decline?
- Which physician segment is likely to generate the highest long-term value?
- Where should additional promotional resources be allocated next quarter?
- Which commercial initiative is most likely to improve organizational performance?

Traditional reporting systems describe what has already happened.

Artificial Intelligence attempts to predict what is likely to happen next.

This distinction represents one of the most significant changes in the history of commercial leadership.

The transition from descriptive management to predictive leadership represents more than a technological improvement. It fundamentally changes how organizations identify risk, allocate resources, prioritize leadership attention, and create sustainable competitive advantage.

Descriptive Management versus Predictive Management

Historically, pharmaceutical organizations have practiced what management scholars describe as **descriptive management**.

Managers reviewed historical performance reports, interpreted trends, discussed results with Regional Managers, and implemented corrective actions after performance problems became visible.

Although this process remains valuable, it is inherently reactive.

Artificial Intelligence introduces the possibility of **predictive management**.

Instead of waiting until performance declines become visible, predictive algorithms identify early warning indicators long before traditional management reports reveal significant problems.

For example, AI systems may recognize subtle changes in physician prescribing behavior, declining customer engagement patterns, territory saturation, coaching effectiveness, or employee performance trajectories months before those trends become evident through conventional reporting.

This enables managers to intervene proactively rather than reactively.

Consequently, leadership becomes increasingly preventive rather than corrective.

Preventive leadership enables organizations to intervene before commercial problems become visible through conventional reporting systems. Rather than reacting to declining performance, leaders continuously shape future outcomes through earlier and more informed decisions.

The New Role of the Field Force Manager

As Artificial Intelligence becomes integrated into pharmaceutical commercial operations, the responsibilities of Field Force Managers will evolve significantly.

Historically, managers primarily supervised activities.

Today, managers increasingly supervise decisions.

Tomorrow, they will supervise decision systems.

This distinction is important.

Artificial Intelligence should never replace managerial accountability.

Instead, it expands managerial capability.

Future commercial leaders will spend less time collecting information and substantially more time interpreting insights, developing people, coaching leaders, managing organizational change, and making strategic business decisions supported by advanced analytical systems.

Therefore, the future Field Force Manager will not simply be expected to understand pharmaceutical sales.

He or she will be expected to understand:

- organizational behavior;
- commercial analytics;
- predictive decision-making;
- digital transformation;
- leadership psychology;
- data interpretation;
- change management; and
- responsible AI governance.

The position itself is evolving from operational supervision toward strategic organizational leadership.

Author's Insight

During my experience managing large pharmaceutical field organizations across multiple regions, I observed that the greatest limitation was rarely the quality of the sales force itself. More often, it was the speed and quality of managerial decision-making.

Regional Managers frequently possessed the necessary information, yet transforming that information into consistent strategic action remained difficult. Weekly reports, monthly dashboards, and quarterly reviews often described problems after they had already affected business performance.

In my view, Artificial Intelligence changes this dynamic. Its greatest contribution is not replacing experienced managers but helping them recognize patterns earlier, prioritize more effectively, and allocate their time to leadership instead of administration.

The organizations that will lead the pharmaceutical industry over the next decade will not necessarily employ the largest sales forces. They will employ the leaders who make the best decisions, supported by the best information.

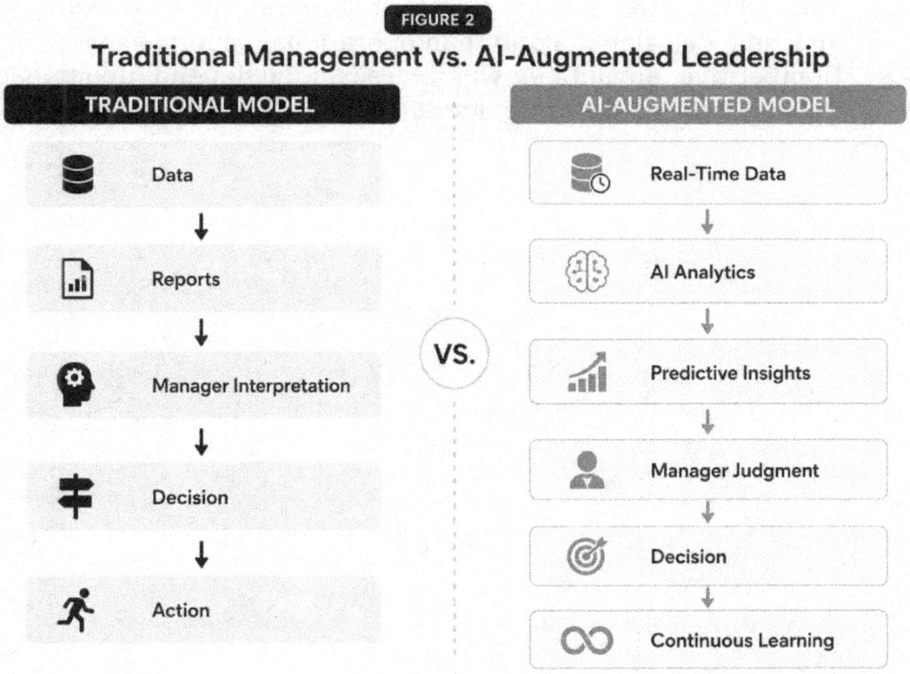

Management Reflection

Before investing in Artificial Intelligence, pharmaceutical organizations should first ask a more fundamental question:

Are we attempting to make existing management processes faster, or are we fundamentally redesigning how commercial decisions are made?

Organizations that merely automate existing processes may improve efficiency.

Organizations that redesign managerial decision-making may redefine competitive advantage (Porter, 1985; Brynjolfsson & McAfee, 2014).

Key Takeaways

- Modern pharmaceutical organizations suffer from **information overload**, not information scarcity.
- Traditional management remains valuable but is increasingly reactive.
- Artificial Intelligence enables predictive, forward-looking leadership.
- The future role of the Field Force Manager will focus more on strategic decision-making than operational supervision.
- Competitive advantage will increasingly depend upon leadership quality supported by intelligent decision systems.

Why Traditional Pharmaceutical Sales Models Are No Longer Enough

---

2.1 The Commercial Model That Built the Pharmaceutical Industry

For more than half a century, pharmaceutical companies achieved remarkable commercial success through a business model centered on personal relationships, scientific promotion, and nationwide field organizations.

Medical Representatives became the primary connection between pharmaceutical manufacturers and healthcare professionals.

The model proved highly successful because it reflected the realities of healthcare delivery at that time.

Physicians relied heavily on face-to-face discussions for scientific updates.

Clinical information traveled relatively slowly.

Product portfolios were smaller.

Competition was less intense.

Regulatory expectations were comparatively limited.

Under these conditions, commercial success largely depended upon four managerial variables:

- Sales force size
- Territory coverage
- Call frequency
- Product knowledge

Organizations continuously expanded field teams because increasing commercial activity generally produced increasing sales performance.

The management philosophy was straightforward:

More representatives generated more physician interactions. More physician interactions generated more prescriptions. More prescriptions generated business growth.

For decades, this model produced exceptional commercial results. Consequently, most pharmaceutical organizations optimized rather than questioned it (Zoltners et al., 2009).

2.2 The Market Has Changed Faster Than Management

The pharmaceutical industry entering the 2030s bears little resemblance to the industry that developed this traditional commercial model.

Healthcare professionals today receive information from dozens of digital sources before meeting a Medical Representative.

Clinical guidelines are updated continuously.

Patients are better informed.

Healthcare systems are increasingly cost-conscious.

Payers demand real-world evidence.

Governments enforce stricter compliance standards.

Digital engagement has become an expected component of customer interaction.

Despite these profound changes, many commercial organizations continue to manage field teams using performance systems originally designed decades ago.

Weekly sales reports remain the primary management tool.

Quarterly business reviews dominate leadership discussions.

Performance evaluations often rely heavily on historical outcomes rather than predictive indicators.

Territories are frequently adjusted after market conditions have already changed.

Training programs are delivered according to annual schedules rather than individual learning needs.

In other words, while the commercial environment has evolved dramatically, many management systems have evolved only incrementally (Kotter, 2012).

2.3 The Hidden Cost of Traditional Management

The limitations of traditional management rarely become visible during periods of market stability.

They become evident during periods of rapid change.

Modern pharmaceutical organizations now face simultaneous challenges that previous generations of leaders rarely encountered:

- shrinking physician access;
- increasing specialty products;
- omnichannel customer engagement;
- expanding compliance requirements;
- rising commercial costs;
- talent shortages;
- increasing employee turnover;
- accelerating scientific innovation.

These factors increase organizational complexity exponentially.

Human managers are expected to process more information, make faster decisions, and coordinate increasingly specialized teams than ever before.

This growing complexity exposes an important reality:

The limiting factor is no longer commercial effort (Davenport & Harris, 2007).

It is managerial capacity.

Organizations do not necessarily require more reports.

They require better decisions.

Author's Insight

During my years leading pharmaceutical field organizations, I observed that commercial performance rarely declined because employees lacked commitment.

More often, performance suffered because managers identified problems too late.

By the time declining productivity appeared in monthly reports, valuable opportunities had already been lost.

Traditional management excels at explaining yesterday.

The future belongs to organizations capable of managing tomorrow.

Artificial Intelligence offers commercial leaders an opportunity to move from retrospective management toward predictive leadership.

That transition may ultimately become the defining competitive advantage of the next generation of pharmaceutical organizations.

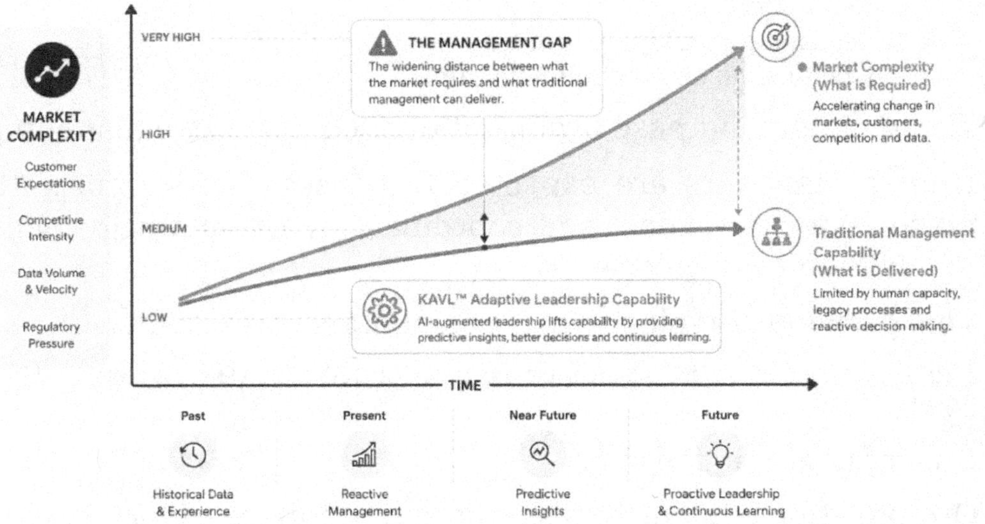

FIGURE 3

THE MANAGEMENT GAP™

As market complexity accelerates, the gap between what traditional management can deliver and what is required continues to widen.

2.4 The New Commercial Reality

The pharmaceutical industry is entering an era characterized not by incremental change, but by continuous disruption. Scientific innovation is accelerating, healthcare delivery models are evolving, regulatory expectations are expanding, and commercial organizations are expected to generate sustainable growth despite increasing operational complexity.

For commercial leaders, this transformation introduces a fundamental management dilemma.

Historically, competitive advantage was achieved primarily through scale. Organizations invested in larger sales forces, broader territorial coverage, greater promotional activity, and increased physician interactions. Growth was largely proportional to organizational expansion.

Today, however, scale alone no longer guarantees commercial success (Porter, 1985; McKinsey & Company, 2025b).

Several structural changes have fundamentally altered the commercial environment.

Healthcare professionals have become significantly more selective regarding interactions with pharmaceutical companies. Digital communication channels have multiplied, reducing dependence on traditional face-to-face engagement. At the same time, healthcare providers increasingly expect personalized scientific information rather than standardized promotional messaging.

Commercial organizations therefore face an unprecedented challenge:

How can fewer interactions generate greater commercial impact?

Answering this question requires a different management philosophy.

Rather than maximizing activity, modern commercial organizations must maximize decision quality (Kahneman, 2011).

The Shift from Activity Management to Intelligence Management

Traditional pharmaceutical management focused primarily on measuring activities.

Managers monitored indicators such as:

- Number of physician visits
- Daily call frequency
- Sales volume
- Product coverage
- Territory activity
- Monthly target achievement

Although these indicators remain valuable, they primarily measure what employees have already completed (Davenport & Harris, 2007).

Artificial Intelligence introduces a fundamentally different perspective.

Instead of asking:

"How many physician visits were completed?"

AI asks:

"Which physician interactions are most likely to generate future clinical engagement?"

Instead of measuring effort,

AI evaluates probability.

Instead of monitoring activity,

AI estimates future outcomes.

Consequently, commercial management begins shifting away from operational supervision toward intelligence-driven leadership.

Information Is No Longer the Competitive Advantage

For decades, pharmaceutical companies competed by possessing superior information.

Medical Representatives served as the primary source of clinical updates for physicians.

Today that reality has changed dramatically.

Healthcare professionals have immediate access to:

- International clinical guidelines
- Scientific journals
- Medical conferences
- Digital education platforms
- Professional communities
- Clinical decision-support systems

Information has become universally accessible.

The competitive advantage has therefore shifted.

The organizations that succeed will not necessarily possess more information. They will possess superior capability for interpreting information (Senge, 2006; Davenport & Harris, 2007).

This distinction is subtle, yet profound.

Artificial Intelligence cannot create scientific evidence.

It cannot replace clinical expertise.

However, it can dramatically improve how commercial organizations interpret available information and convert that knowledge into strategic decisions.

Consequently, AI should be viewed primarily as an organizational intelligence platform instead of merely another digital technology (Russell & Norvig, 2021).

FIGURE 4

EVOLUTION OF COMPETITIVE ADVANTAGE

The source of sustainable advantage has shifted with each era.
Leaders who adapt to the next shift define the future.

1950s

INFORMATION ADVANTAGE

Access to information was limited and controlled. Organizations that had the information held the advantage.

↓

1980s

SALES FORCE ADVANTAGE

The strength, size and motivation of the sales force became the primary driver of market success. Reach and frequency created value.

↓

2000s

CUSTOMER RELATIONSHIP ADVANTAGE

Strong relationships, trust and service quality differentiated leading companies. Customer centricity created loyalty.

↓

2020s

DATA ADVANTAGE

Data became abundant and measurable. Organizations that could collect, integrate and analyze data gained superior insights.

↓

2030+

DECISION INTELLIGENCE ADVANTAGE

The ability to turn data and insights into better, faster and smarter decisions will become the ultimate source of sustainable advantage.

The future belongs to organizations that combine data, technology and human judgment to make better decisions continuously and at scale.

2.5 The Emerging Commercial Leadership Model

One of the most significant consequences of Artificial Intelligence is not technological.

It is organizational.

As predictive technologies become increasingly integrated into commercial operations, the expectations placed upon commercial leaders change fundamentally.

Historically, successful managers were expected to possess extensive product knowledge, strong interpersonal skills, and operational discipline (Mintzberg, 1973; Drucker, 2007).

Tomorrow's commercial leaders will continue to require these competencies.

However, additional capabilities will become equally important.

Future pharmaceutical leaders must be capable of:

- interpreting predictive analytics;
- evaluating AI-generated recommendations;
- understanding algorithmic limitations;
- integrating commercial judgment with machine intelligence;
- leading organizational change;
- maintaining ethical oversight of AI-assisted decisions (Heifetz et al., 2009; Senge, 2006).

This represents the emergence of a new leadership profile.

Technology does not eliminate leadership.

It increases the value of leadership.

The most successful pharmaceutical organizations will therefore be those capable of combining experienced human judgment with intelligent analytical systems.

Commercial excellence will increasingly become the result of this partnership.

EXECUTIVE PERSPECTIVE

Leading Organizational Growth During Commercial Expansion

Throughout my leadership career, I discovered that managing organizational growth is fundamentally different from managing sales growth.

During one international leadership assignment, I was responsible for a nationwide pharmaceutical commercial organization consisting of more than **140 Medical Representatives** and over **20 Regional Managers**. During the same period, the organization experienced significant commercial expansion, with annual retail sales increasing from approximately **USD 19.6 million** to more than **USD 43.5 million**.

From the outside, this appeared to be a commercial success story.

From the inside, however, it was primarily a leadership challenge.

As commercial performance accelerated, organizational complexity increased even faster. More managers required coaching. Cross-functional collaboration became increasingly important. Territory structures needed continuous refinement. Performance reviews became more sophisticated, while expectations from senior leadership continued to rise.

One observation became increasingly clear.

Commercial growth does not automatically create organizational capability.

In fact, rapid commercial expansion often exposes weaknesses that remain invisible during periods of stable growth.

Weekly reports became longer.

Performance dashboards became more detailed.

Additional KPIs were introduced.

Yet despite having more information than ever before, managers often struggled to determine which actions deserved immediate attention.

The limiting factor was no longer information.

The limiting factor was managerial capacity.

Looking back, I believe this experience fundamentally changed my understanding of leadership.

The role of a commercial leader is not to review every report or supervise every activity. The role of a leader is to recognize meaningful patterns, make timely decisions, develop future leaders, and maintain organizational alignment as complexity increases.

Today, Artificial Intelligence offers an opportunity to strengthen each of these responsibilities.

AI can process information at a scale impossible for human managers.

It can identify hidden relationships across commercial datasets.

It can prioritize opportunities and highlight emerging risks.

However, it cannot replace leadership.

Technology may accelerate analysis, but only experienced leaders can interpret organizational context, balance competing priorities, and make decisions that consider both business performance and people.

This experience ultimately shaped one of the central ideas presented throughout this book:

Sustainable commercial success depends less on organizational size and more on leadership quality supported by intelligent decision-making.

Leadership Reflection

One of the most valuable lessons I learned is that organizational complexity grows faster than commercial performance.

Increasing sales is challenging.

Building an organization capable of sustaining that growth is even more difficult.

Artificial Intelligence can help leaders understand complexity.

Only leadership can transform complexity into coordinated action.

Author's Insight

During my leadership career, I learned that successful pharmaceutical organizations rarely outperform competitors because they collect more data.

They outperform competitors because their leaders ask better questions.

Artificial Intelligence does not change this principle.

Instead, it enables leaders to ask more sophisticated questions, evaluate more alternatives, and make decisions supported by substantially greater analytical capability.

Technology expands the decision space.

Leadership determines how that space is used.

Management Reflection

Question for Commercial Leaders

If Artificial Intelligence can analyze every commercial report within seconds,

what becomes the most valuable responsibility of a Field Force Manager?

The answer is no longer reporting.

The answer is leadership.

Key Takeaways

- Scale is no longer the primary driver of competitive advantage.
- Commercial success increasingly depends on decision quality.
- Information is becoming a commodity; interpretation is becoming the differentiator.
- AI should augment—not replace—managerial judgment.
- Future pharmaceutical leaders will need both commercial expertise and analytical literacy.

3.1 Artificial Intelligence Is Changing Commercial Organizations

Artificial Intelligence has rapidly evolved from an experimental technology into a strategic capability that is transforming nearly every function within the pharmaceutical industry. While early investments focused primarily on drug discovery, clinical development, and regulatory automation, commercial organizations are increasingly emerging as one of the most significant beneficiaries of AI adoption.

Recent industry analyses indicate that commercial functions—including sales, marketing, customer engagement, field enablement, and market access—represent one of the largest opportunities for AI-driven value creation within life sciences organizations. McKinsey estimates that generative AI alone could create USD 18-30 billion in annual value for commercial functions, out of a broader estimated USD 60–110 billion in annual value across the pharmaceutical and medical products industries (McKinsey & Company, 2024a).

This finding reflects a fundamental reality.

Unlike research laboratories or manufacturing facilities, commercial organizations generate enormous volumes of continuously changing information:

- physician engagement
- customer segmentation
- prescription trends
- CRM interactions
- omnichannel activity
- territory performance
- reimbursement changes
- competitive intelligence
- marketing effectiveness
- sales forecasting

Historically, these datasets existed independently.

Artificial Intelligence enables organizations to integrate them into a single decision-support ecosystem.

3.2 From Data Collection to Decision Intelligence

The pharmaceutical industry has invested billions of dollars over the past two decades in Customer Relationship Management (CRM) platforms, Business Intelligence systems, enterprise resource planning software, omnichannel engagement platforms, and advanced analytics solutions.

However, collecting data has never been the ultimate objective.

The real objective is improving decision quality.

Many organizations continue to produce hundreds of commercial reports every month, yet senior managers frequently struggle to answer relatively simple questions:

- Which physicians are most likely to increase prescribing over the next six months?
- Which Medical Representatives require immediate coaching?
- Which Regional Managers demonstrate the highest leadership potential?
- Which territories require restructuring before commercial performance declines?
- Which marketing activities generate measurable improvements in physician engagement?

Traditional analytics describe historical performance.

Artificial Intelligence attempts to estimate future outcomes (IQVIA, 2024).

This distinction represents the transition from **Business Intelligence** toward **Decision Intelligence**, a management philosophy in which predictive analytics actively support managerial judgment instead of simply reporting historical events.

According to IQVIA, modern commercial organizations increasingly require connected data, AI-driven analytics, and real-time insights capable of supporting faster, more confident commercial decisions across the entire product lifecycle.

3.3 Why Pharmaceutical Commercial Organizations Are Especially Suitable for AI

Not every business function benefits equally from Artificial Intelligence.

Commercial organizations possess several characteristics that make them particularly suitable for predictive analytics.

First, they generate extremely large volumes of structured and unstructured data.

Every physician visit, CRM interaction, sales transaction, customer inquiry, digital engagement, marketing campaign, and field coaching session creates information that can contribute to future decision-making.

Second, commercial organizations operate in highly dynamic environments.

Market access policies change.

Competitors launch new products.

Physician behavior evolves.

Healthcare regulations are updated.

Patient expectations continue to increase.

Traditional management often struggles to respond rapidly to these changes.

Artificial Intelligence significantly increases organizational responsiveness by continuously monitoring evolving commercial patterns and identifying emerging opportunities before they become visible through conventional reporting systems (Davenport & Harris, 2007).

Third, pharmaceutical commercial organizations depend heavily upon resource allocation.

Every decision regarding territory alignment, sales force deployment, coaching priorities, promotional investments, and customer engagement carries financial consequences.

AI enables leaders to optimize these decisions using significantly larger datasets than human managers could realistically evaluate.

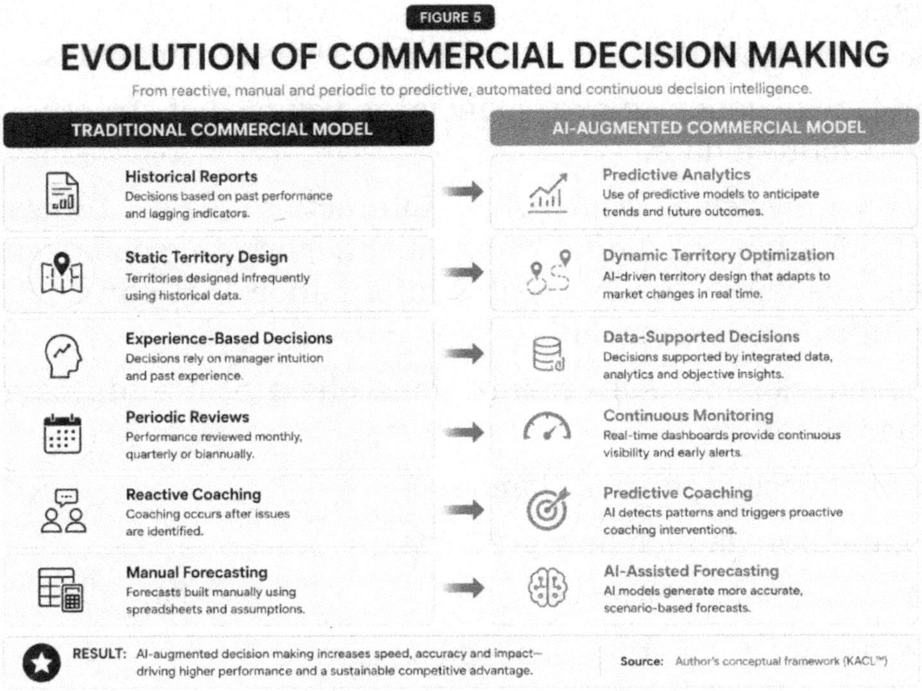

3.4 AI Does Not Replace Commercial Leadership

One of the most common misconceptions surrounding Artificial Intelligence is the belief that algorithms will eventually replace commercial managers.

Current evidence suggests the opposite.

Organizations achieving the greatest value from AI are those that combine advanced analytical capabilities with experienced human leadership instead of attempting to automate managerial judgment entirely. McKinsey's research on life sciences organizations found that many companies have experimented with generative AI, but only a small minority have successfully scaled it into a consistent competitive advantage. The differentiating factor is not access to AI itself; it is organizational readiness, leadership alignment, and the ability to integrate AI into business processes (McKinsey & Company, 2025a).

Artificial Intelligence is exceptionally effective at identifying patterns (Russell & Norvig, 2021).

Managers remain responsible for understanding context.

AI estimates probability.

Leaders evaluate consequences.

AI recommends actions.

Leaders make decisions.

This distinction is particularly important within pharmaceutical organizations, where commercial decisions frequently involve regulatory, ethical, scientific, and organizational considerations that extend beyond numerical optimization.

Consequently, the future role of Field Force Managers will become increasingly strategic.

Routine analytical tasks may become automated.

Leadership will not.

Instead, leadership responsibilities will expand toward:

- organizational transformation;
- strategic coaching;
- cross-functional coordination;
- change management;
- ethical governance of AI-supported decisions;
- and long-term commercial capability building.

EXECUTIVE PERSPECTIVE

When Curiosity Becomes Competitive Advantage

One of the most valuable leadership lessons I learned throughout my commercial career was that sustainable innovation rarely begins with technology.

It begins with understanding human behavior.

During one commercial initiative, our leadership team faced a familiar challenge.

Medical Representatives were conducting high-quality scientific discussions with physicians, yet those conversations often ended when the representative left the clinic. Valuable scientific information was available, but opportunities for continued engagement were limited.

Instead of asking how we could increase the number of promotional visits, we asked a different question:

How can scientific engagement continue after the face-to-face interaction has ended?

Because pharmaceutical promotion operated under strict regulatory limitations, traditional promotional materials offered limited opportunities to extend communication. This challenge encouraged us to think differently.

We developed a dedicated educational website containing scientific information that healthcare professionals could access independently after the visit. Medical Representatives introduced the platform through a simple QR code that provided immediate access without requiring printed promotional materials.

The technology itself, however, was only one part of the solution.

The more important innovation focused on human curiosity.

Instead of displaying product names or promotional messages, our field team used apparel featuring only the molecular structure of the active pharmaceutical ingredient. The design intentionally avoided promotional claims while presenting a scientific symbol that physicians and pharmacists immediately recognized as unusual.

The response was remarkable.

Healthcare professionals frequently initiated the conversation themselves by asking,

"Which molecule is this?"

That single question transformed the interaction.

Instead of beginning with product promotion, conversations naturally evolved into scientific discussion driven by professional curiosity.

This subtle shift fundamentally changed the quality of engagement.

The project continued for approximately three months.

During the implementation year, annual commercial sales increased from approximately 69 million to 165 million (local currency). Although multiple organizational and market factors contributed to this overall business growth, the experience demonstrated that thoughtfully designed customer engagement strategies can meaningfully support commercial performance when integrated with disciplined field execution and scientific credibility.

Looking back, I realized that the greatest innovation was not the QR code.

Nor was it the website.

The true innovation was designing an experience that encouraged healthcare professionals to ask the first question.

Today, Artificial Intelligence expands this principle even further.

AI can personalize educational journeys, recommend relevant scientific content, identify engagement preferences, and optimize communication timing. Yet even the most advanced technology cannot replace the human motivations that drive learning.

Curiosity remains human.

Trust remains human.

Leadership is responsible for designing experiences that connect both.

Leadership Reflection

Technology attracts attention.

Curiosity creates engagement.

Scientific value builds trust.

Sustainable commercial innovation emerges when leaders understand how these three elements work together—not as isolated tactics, but as an integrated customer experience.

Author's Insight

During my years leading large pharmaceutical field organizations, I often observed that commercial discussions were dominated by historical performance reports. By the time a declining trend became visible, opportunities had already been lost.

Artificial Intelligence changes the timing of management.

Instead of asking managers to explain yesterday's performance, AI enables them to anticipate tomorrow's challenges.

This shift fundamentally changes the role of commercial leadership.

Leaders become architects of future performance rather than reviewers of historical results.

Management Reflection

Leadership Question

If Artificial Intelligence can continuously analyze every physician interaction, commercial KPI, CRM activity, and sales trend in real time,

what becomes the highest-value activity of a pharmaceutical Field Force Manager?

Perhaps the answer is no longer supervising activities.

Perhaps it is developing people, shaping organizational culture, and making better strategic decisions supported by intelligent systems.

Key Takeaways

- Artificial Intelligence is becoming a strategic capability across pharmaceutical commercial organizations.
- The greatest commercial value of AI lies in improving decision quality rather than automating routine tasks.
- Pharmaceutical commercial organizations are particularly well suited to AI because of their large, continuously evolving datasets.
- Organizations that combine experienced leadership with AI-enabled analytics are more likely to achieve sustainable commercial excellence than organizations relying on either human judgment or automation alone.
- The future of pharmaceutical commercial leadership will depend upon integrating managerial expertise with predictive decision-support systems.

THE KAVUN ADAPTIVE COMMERCIAL LEADERSHIP FRAMEWORK™ (KACL)

Reimagining Pharmaceutical Commercial Leadership in the Age of Artificial Intelligence

---

4.1 Introduction

Artificial Intelligence has generated unprecedented enthusiasm across the pharmaceutical industry. Most discussions, however, remain focused on technological capabilities rather than organizational transformation (Deloitte, 2024; McKinsey & Company, 2024b).

Existing literature largely examines AI through the perspectives of drug discovery, clinical development, manufacturing, pharmacovigilance, and commercial productivity. McKinsey, for example, estimates that generative AI can unlock USD 18–30 billion annually in commercial value for pharmaceutical and medical products organizations, while emphasizing that sustainable impact depends not merely on technology adoption but on organizational readiness, leadership alignment, and scalable implementation (McKinsey & Company, 2024a) (McKinsey & Company, 2024a).

Despite this growing body of research, a fundamental question remains insufficiently explored:

How should pharmaceutical commercial leadership itself evolve in response to Artificial Intelligence?

Most publications describe what AI can do.

Very few describe how commercial leaders should change (Senge, 2006).

This chapter introduces **The Kavun Adaptive Commercial Leadership Framework (KACL Framework[1])** as a conceptual model designed to bridge this gap.

Unlike technology-centered models, the KACL Framework positions leadership—not Artificial Intelligence—as the primary driver of commercial excellence.

Artificial Intelligence is treated as an organizational capability that enhances managerial decision-making, organizational learning, and commercial execution, while human leaders remain accountable for strategy, ethics,

---

[1] The KACL Framework™ is an original conceptual leadership framework developed by the author to integrate human leadership, organizational intelligence, and Artificial Intelligence within pharmaceutical commercial organizations. The framework is introduced in this publication to encourage further academic discussion, empirical validation, and practical application.

people development, and organizational culture (Davenport & Harris, 2007; Brynjolfsson & McAfee, 2014).

4.2 Why Existing Leadership Models Need to Evolve

Traditional pharmaceutical leadership has historically been built upon four fundamental assumptions: (Drucker, 2007).

- Managers possess superior experience.
- Historical performance predicts future performance.
- Standardized management practices produce standardized outcomes.
- Human judgment represents the primary source of competitive advantage.

These assumptions served the pharmaceutical industry remarkably well for decades (Zoltners et al., 2009).

However, commercial organizations entering the AI era operate under fundamentally different conditions (Brynjolfsson & McAfee, 2014; McKinsey & Company, 2025a).

Commercial leaders now manage:

- exponentially larger datasets;
- omnichannel customer engagement;
- increasingly specialized therapeutic portfolios;
- continuously changing healthcare ecosystems;
- greater regulatory expectations;
- faster competitive cycles;
- geographically distributed commercial organizations.

Consequently, leadership itself becomes increasingly dependent upon the ability to interpret complexity instead of merely supervise activity (Davenport & Harris, 2007).

Research published by McKinsey indicates that organizations successfully scaling generative AI differ not because they possess superior technology, but because leadership actively redesigns business processes, governance structures, and decision-making models around AI capabilities. Organizations that simply deploy AI tools without changing management practices rarely achieve meaningful competitive differentiation (McKinsey & Company, 2025a).

This observation forms the conceptual foundation of the KACL Framework.

4.3 The Philosophy Behind the KACL Framework

The central proposition of the KACL Framework is straightforward:

Artificial Intelligence should amplify leadership—not replace it.

Commercial excellence results from the interaction of three organizational capabilities:

1. Human Leadership
2. Organizational Intelligence
3. Artificial Intelligence

None of these capabilities independently creates sustainable competitive advantage.

Leadership without data becomes intuition.

Data without leadership becomes noise.

Artificial Intelligence without organizational purpose becomes automation.

Only when these three elements interact continuously can pharmaceutical organizations achieve adaptive commercial excellence.

Accordingly, the KACL Framework rejects two common misconceptions.

The first misconception assumes that AI will replace commercial managers.

The second assumes that experienced leaders alone can manage future organizational complexity without AI support.

Neither assumption reflects current evidence (McKinsey & Company, 2025; Deloitte, 2025).

Instead, AI should function as an organizational intelligence layer supporting managerial judgment while preserving human accountability (OECD, 2024; World Health Organization, 2021).

FIGURE 6

THE KACL FRAMEWORK™

The integration of human leadership, organizational intelligence and artificial intelligence drives sustainable commercial excellence.

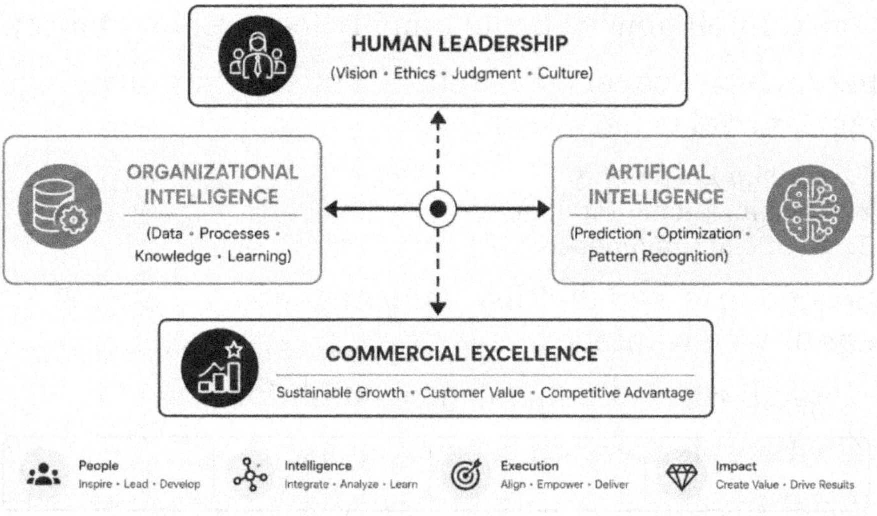

Source: Author's conceptual framework (KACL™)

4.4 The Five Pillars of Adaptive Commercial Leadership

The KACL Framework proposes that future pharmaceutical commercial organizations should be developed around five mutually reinforcing leadership capabilities.

Pillar I — Strategic Vision

Commercial leaders remain responsible for defining organizational direction (Drucker, 2007).

Artificial Intelligence can evaluate scenarios, estimate probabilities, and recommend alternatives.

Only leadership determines organizational purpose.

Vision remains fundamentally human (Kotter, 2012).

Pillar II — Predictive Decision Intelligence

Managers should transition from descriptive management toward predictive management (Davenport & Harris, 2007).

Rather than asking:

"What happened?"

leaders increasingly ask:

"What is most likely to happen next?" (Kahneman, 2011).

Predictive analytics support this transition by continuously evaluating commercial signals before they become operational problems.

This concept aligns with current industry recommendations emphasizing AI-assisted commercial planning and decision support (McKinsey & Company, 2025; IQVIA, 2024).

Pillar III — Adaptive Organizational Learning

Traditional organizations learn periodically (Senge, 2006).

Adaptive organizations learn continuously (Senge, 2006).

Every physician interaction.

Every CRM entry.

Every coaching session.

Every territory adjustment.

Every sales forecast.

Every commercial campaign.

becomes organizational knowledge (Argyris & Schön, 1978; Senge, 2006).

Artificial Intelligence accelerates this learning cycle by identifying hidden relationships across large commercial datasets (Davenport & Harris, 2007; Senge, 2006).

Pillar IV — Human-Centered Leadership

Despite rapid technological progress, pharmaceutical organizations remain fundamentally human organizations (Drucker, 2007).

Medical Representatives require coaching.

Regional Managers require mentoring.

Teams require motivation.

Culture requires trust. (Goleman et al., 2013)

Artificial Intelligence cannot replace these responsibilities (Russell & Norvig, 2021).

Instead, it creates additional time for leaders to focus on them (Brynjolfsson & McAfee, 2014).

Pillar V — Ethical Governance

Commercial decisions within healthcare possess ethical consequences extending beyond financial performance (World Health Organization, 2021).

Responsible AI governance therefore becomes a core leadership responsibility (OECD, 2024).

Managers must ensure that AI-supported recommendations remain transparent, explainable, compliant, scientifically appropriate, and aligned with patient interests (OECD, 2024; World Health Organization, 2021).

This principle is also consistent with internationally recognized AI governance frameworks published by organizations such as the OECD and WHO, which emphasize transparency, accountability, fairness, and human oversight in AI-enabled decision-making (OECD, 2024; World Health Organization, 2021).

Author's Insight

During more than two decades leading pharmaceutical commercial organizations, I gradually realized that the greatest competitive advantage was never superior products alone.

It was the ability of leaders to transform uncertainty into informed decisions.

Artificial Intelligence does not eliminate uncertainty.

It reduces it.

Leadership remains responsible for everything that technology cannot measure:

trust,

purpose,

culture,

ethics,

and the courage to make difficult decisions.

That realization ultimately became the foundation of the KACL Framework.

AI-ENABLED TERRITORY LEADERSHIP

Applying the KACL Framework to Territory Strategy, Field Execution, and Commercial Performance

---

5.1 Introduction

Territory management has long been recognized as one of the most influential determinants of pharmaceutical commercial performance. For decades, pharmaceutical companies have invested substantial resources in designing territories that balance physician coverage, market potential, travel efficiency, and sales force workload. Although territory alignment has traditionally been viewed as an operational exercise, it is increasingly becoming a strategic capability that directly influences customer engagement, resource allocation, forecasting accuracy, and organizational productivity (Zoltners et al., 2009; Piercy & Lane, 2009).

Historically, territory design relied on periodic reviews supported by historical prescription data, geographic boundaries, physician segmentation, and managerial experience. While these approaches produced acceptable results in relatively stable markets, they are increasingly inadequate within today's rapidly evolving healthcare environment (Zoltners et al., 2009).

Healthcare professionals continuously change prescribing behaviors. Market access restrictions evolve. Competitors launch new therapies. Digital engagement channels expand. Patient demographics shift. Scientific evidence develops rapidly. Consequently, territory designs that remain static for twelve months may become misaligned with commercial realities long before the next annual planning cycle (IQVIA, 2024).

Recent McKinsey research argues that commercial organizations capable of integrating AI into core commercial processes are moving beyond isolated automation projects toward **domain-level transformation**, where AI continuously improves decision-making across the commercial organization instead of simply accelerating existing workflows.

This chapter proposes that territory management should be viewed not as a geographic optimization problem but as a continuous leadership process supported by predictive intelligence.

5.2 The Evolution of Territory Management

Territory management has evolved through four distinct generations.

Generation One: Geographic Coverage

The earliest pharmaceutical territory models were based almost exclusively on geography. Representatives were assigned territories according to cities, administrative regions, or travel convenience. Success depended primarily on maximizing physician coverage (Zoltners et al., 2009).

Management questions included:

- How many physicians are covered?
- How frequently are they visited?
- How large is the territory?

The underlying assumption was simple:

Greater coverage produces greater commercial opportunity.

Generation Two: Potential-Based Segmentation

As CRM systems matured, pharmaceutical companies began incorporating physician potential into territory design (Payne & Frow, 2005).

Organizations classified physicians according to prescription volume, specialty, patient population, and commercial value.

Managers no longer attempted to visit every physician equally.

Instead, they prioritized high-value customer segments.

This represented a significant improvement.

However, territory structures remained relatively static.

They still depended primarily upon historical information.

Generation Three: Data-Driven Optimization

Business Intelligence platforms introduced substantially larger datasets (Davenport & Harris, 2007).

Organizations began considering:

- prescription trends;
- call effectiveness;
- travel efficiency;
- physician responsiveness;
- market share;

- reimbursement dynamics.

Territory decisions became increasingly analytical.

Nevertheless, managers still relied upon historical performance.

The question remained:

What happened?

Generation Four: AI-Augmented Territory Leadership

Artificial Intelligence fundamentally changes the objective of territory management (Russell & Norvig, 2021).

Rather than describing existing territory performance, AI continuously evaluates future commercial opportunities.

Instead of asking:

"Which territory generated the highest sales?"

leaders increasingly ask:

- Which territory is most likely to underperform next quarter?
- Which physician relationships require immediate attention?
- Which representative should receive additional coaching?
- Which territory should be redesigned before commercial performance declines?

The managerial objective therefore shifts from optimization toward anticipation (Davenport & Harris, 2007).

FIGURE 7

EVOLUTION OF TERRITORY MANAGEMENT

Territory management has evolved from geographic coverage to predictive intelligence, driving future performance and sustainable competitive advantage.

GENERATION	PRIMARY DRIVER	MANAGEMENT FOCUS
1 Geographic Coverage 1950s–1970s	Geography	Coverage
2 Potential Segmentation 1970s–1990s	Physician Value	Prioritization
3 Data-Driven Optimization 1990s–2020s	Historical Analytics	Performance
4 AI-Augmented Leadership 2020s–2030+	Predictive Intelligence	Future Performance

The evolution from static territories to AI-augmented, predictive territories enables organizations to deploy resources more effectively, improve customer engagement and accelerate growth.

Source: Author's conceptual framework (KACL™)

5.3 Why Traditional Territory Design Is No Longer Enough

Most pharmaceutical companies continue to redesign territories periodically—often once or twice per year.

This practice reflects an implicit assumption that market conditions remain relatively stable between planning cycles.

Increasingly, this assumption no longer holds.

Commercial environments evolve continuously (McKinsey & Company, 2025a).

Examples include:

- New clinical guidelines
- Competitor launches
- Changes in reimbursement policy
- Physician retirement or relocation
- Shifts in patient demographics
- Growth of digital engagement
- Emerging hospital networks

By the time traditional planning processes identify these changes, the commercial opportunity may already have shifted (Kotter, 2012).

McKinsey's commercial life sciences research emphasizes that organizations creating measurable value from generative AI are redesigning commercial workflows instead of simply automating existing reporting processes. Successful companies embed AI directly into commercial planning and execution instead of treating it as a stand-alone analytics tool.

5.4 Applying the KACL Framework

The KACL Framework proposes that territory leadership should integrate three continuously interacting capabilities:

Human Leadership

Responsible for:

- commercial strategy;
- coaching;
- organizational priorities;
- ethical judgment;
- stakeholder management.

Organizational Intelligence

Responsible for:

- CRM data;
- physician segmentation;
- historical performance;
- commercial processes;
- organizational learning.

Artificial Intelligence

Responsible for:

- predictive analytics;
- pattern recognition;
- opportunity identification;
- forecasting;
- scenario simulation;
- optimization recommendations.

Only when these three capabilities operate together can territory management become adaptive and less reactive.

EXECUTIVE PERSPECTIVE

Coordinating Scientific Field Execution Across a Nationwide Organization

One of the most valuable leadership experiences in my career did not involve launching a new product or achieving an aggressive sales target. Instead, it involved coordinating a nationwide scientific education initiative across a large commercial organization.

The objective was straightforward but highly demanding: deliver consistent, evidence-based scientific information to healthcare professionals through a coordinated field effort while maintaining the highest standards of scientific integrity and operational consistency.

The initiative ultimately included **more than 50 scientific educational meetings** and reached **over 3,500 physicians** through structured scientific engagement.

Although the scientific content was developed centrally, successful implementation depended almost entirely on leadership execution.

Regional managers needed to align local teams around common objectives. Field representatives required consistent training. Medical experts, commercial leaders, and support functions had to coordinate their activities despite different priorities and responsibilities.

As the project expanded, I realized that the greatest challenge was not organizing meetings.

The greatest challenge was ensuring that every team interpreted the strategy in the same way and executed it with the same level of quality.

Leadership, in this context, became an exercise in organizational alignment rather than operational control.

Looking back, this experience closely reflects the principles presented in the KACL Framework.

Human leadership provided strategic direction, coaching, and organizational alignment.

Organizational intelligence supplied the operational data, planning processes, and execution standards.

If today's Artificial Intelligence capabilities had been available at that time, they could have significantly improved resource planning, participation forecasting, scheduling efficiency, and early identification of implementation risks.

However, one conclusion remains unchanged.

Technology can coordinate activities.

Only leadership can align people around a shared purpose.

The experience reinforced my belief that sustainable commercial excellence is achieved when organizational systems and human leadership evolve together—not when one attempts to replace the other.

Leadership Reflection

Large organizations rarely fail because of a lack of information (Davenport & Harris, 2007).

They struggle when information is interpreted differently across teams (Senge, 2006).

One of the most important responsibilities of leadership is creating a common understanding that allows hundreds of people to move in the same direction with consistency and purpose.

FIGURE 8

AI-ENABLED TERRITORY LEADERSHIP CYCLE

A continuous, data-driven cycle that turns insights into actions
and actions into better results.

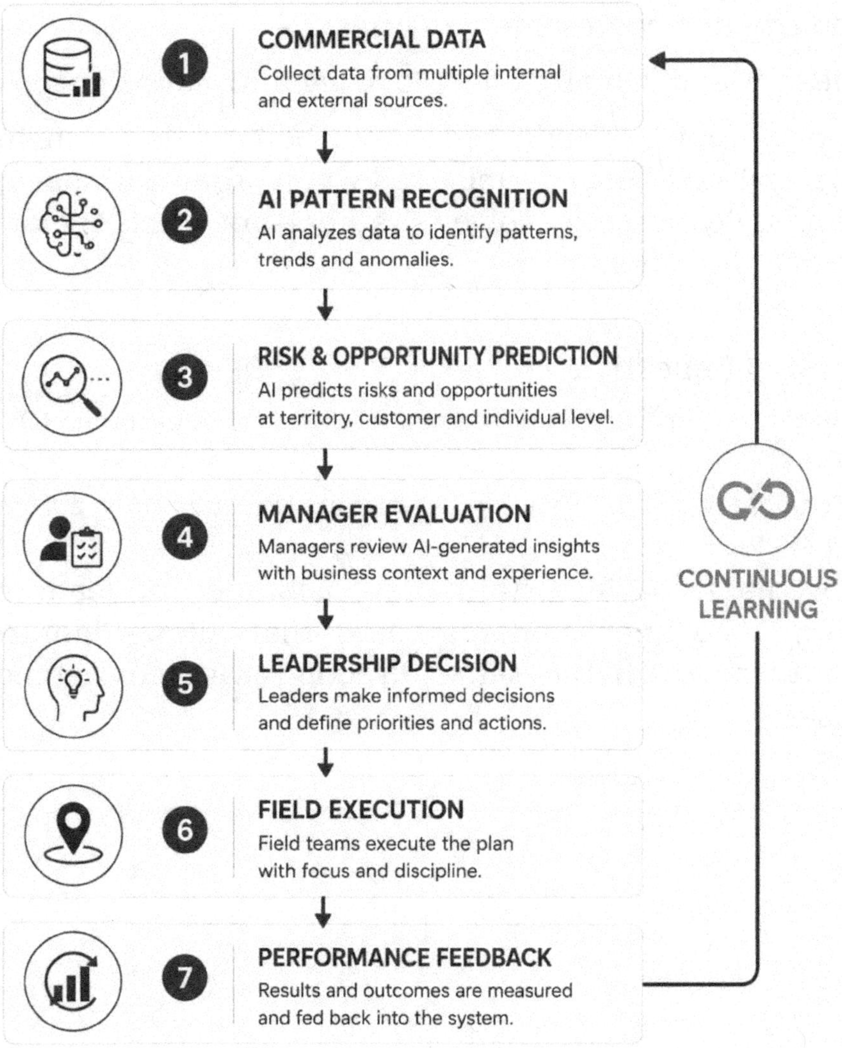

This cycle creates a self-improving system where every decision makes the next decision smarter.

Source: Author's conceptual framework (KACL™)

5.5 Case Study (Illustrative Scenario)

Consider a national pharmaceutical organization responsible for approximately 140 Medical Representatives across multiple regions.

Historically, territory reviews were conducted quarterly. Managers relied on sales reports, CRM summaries, and field observations to identify underperforming territories.

Under an AI-enabled approach, the commercial dashboard identifies that one region has a **high probability of missing its quarterly objective** based on multiple converging indicators:

- declining engagement with high-value physicians;
- reduced follow-up after scientific meetings;
- increased competitive activity;
- lower coaching frequency for the Regional Manager;
- changes in referral patterns.

Instead of waiting for quarterly sales results, the system recommends immediate interventions:

- targeted coaching for the Regional Manager;
- temporary reallocation of promotional resources;
- revised physician prioritization;
- updated call plans;
- additional omnichannel engagement for selected healthcare professionals.

The commercial leader reviews these recommendations, considers contextual factors, and decides which interventions should be implemented.

The decision remains human.

The intelligence becomes augmented.

This approach aligns with McKinsey's observation that AI creates the greatest value when embedded directly into business workflows and leadership decisions rather than deployed as isolated productivity tools.

AI-DRIVEN LEADERSHIP COACHING

Transforming Regional Manager Development Through Artificial Intelligence

---

6.1 Leadership Development Is Becoming the New Competitive Advantage

Throughout the history of the pharmaceutical industry, commercial excellence has traditionally been associated with product innovation, market access, physician engagement, and sales execution. While these capabilities remain essential, the accelerating complexity of today's healthcare environment is shifting competitive advantage toward another dimension that has historically received less strategic attention: (Porter, 1985; Zoltners et al., 2009).

Leadership capability.

Commercial organizations no longer compete solely through products or promotional investments. They increasingly compete through the quality of decisions made by leaders at every level of the organization (Drucker, 2007; Davenport & Harris, 2007).

Regional Managers, Field Force Managers, Commercial Directors, and Business Unit Leaders collectively shape thousands of operational decisions every week. These decisions influence physician engagement, customer prioritization, coaching effectiveness, resource allocation, organizational culture, employee retention, and ultimately commercial performance (Mintzberg, 1973).

The effectiveness of these leaders therefore represents a strategic asset instead of simply a human resource function (Barney, 1991).

Recent McKinsey research argues that the organizations achieving the greatest value from AI are redesigning how managers work instead of merely introducing new technology. AI enables managers to spend less time diagnosing performance and more time coaching, developing talent, and leading organizational change.

This represents a profound shift.

Artificial Intelligence should not primarily be viewed as a tool for replacing managerial work (Russell & Norvig, 2021).

It should be viewed as a catalyst for improving leadership quality (Davenport & Harris, 2007).

6.2 Why Traditional Coaching Models No Longer Scale

Traditional pharmaceutical coaching follows a familiar rhythm.

Regional Managers accompany Medical Representatives during field visits.

Field Force Managers periodically accompany Regional Managers.

Commercial Directors conduct quarterly business reviews.

Annual performance evaluations summarize overall leadership effectiveness.

Although this model has supported commercial organizations for decades, it presents several structural limitations (Kotter, 2012).

First, coaching opportunities are inherently limited.

A Field Force Manager responsible for twenty Regional Managers cannot directly observe every leadership interaction occurring across the organization.

Second, coaching quality varies considerably according to managerial experience.

Some Regional Managers receive exceptional developmental feedback, while others receive little beyond operational direction.

Third, feedback is often retrospective.

By the time coaching occurs, the leadership behaviors influencing organizational performance may already have produced measurable consequences.

These limitations become increasingly significant as organizations grow larger and commercial environments become more dynamic.

Traditional coaching therefore struggles to scale proportionally with organizational complexity (Senge, 2006).

6.3 Artificial Intelligence as a Leadership Multiplier

Artificial Intelligence introduces an entirely different coaching paradigm (Russell & Norvig, 2021).

Instead of relying exclusively upon periodic observation, AI enables continuous leadership intelligence (Davenport & Harris, 2007).

Every leadership interaction generates information (Davenport & Harris, 2007).

Examples include:

- CRM usage patterns
- Coaching frequency
- Territory review quality
- One-to-one meeting cadence
- Performance trend consistency
- Employee engagement indicators
- Training completion
- Call planning quality
- Forecast accuracy
- Team turnover

Individually, these indicators provide only partial insight.

Collectively, they create a comprehensive leadership profile (Senge, 2006).

AI systems continuously evaluate these signals and identify patterns that may indicate emerging leadership strengths or potential developmental needs (Russell & Norvig, 2021; Davenport & Harris, 2007).

Importantly, AI does not evaluate personality.

It evaluates leadership behaviors (Sinha et al., 2024).

This distinction preserves human judgment while improving managerial visibility.

Harvard Business Review describes AI assistants as digital coaches capable of analyzing conversations, identifying behavioral patterns, and delivering personalized developmental feedback. The authors emphasize that AI is most valuable when it augments—not replaces—human coaching relationships.

EXECUTIVE PERSPECTIVE

Developing Future Leaders Instead of Managing Current Performance

One of the most significant leadership lessons I learned throughout my career was that managing performance and developing leaders are fundamentally different responsibilities.

Performance management focuses on today's results.

Leadership development focuses on tomorrow's organization.

While leading a large commercial field organization, I quickly realized that the strongest regional managers were not always those responsible for the highest sales results. In many cases, the individuals who generated the greatest long-term organizational value were those who consistently developed capable teams, coached future leaders, and created environments where performance could be sustained.

This observation gradually changed the way I evaluated leadership.

Instead of asking only "*Who achieved the best results?*" I began asking a different question:

"Who is developing the next generation of leaders?"

That single change significantly improved the quality of leadership discussions throughout the organization.

Performance indicators remained important, but they became only one component of leadership evaluation.

Equal attention was given to coaching quality, succession planning, employee development, collaboration, and organizational learning.

These factors rarely appeared in traditional performance dashboards.

Nevertheless, they often determined whether commercial success would continue over the following years.

Artificial Intelligence now offers an opportunity to strengthen this process.

Behavioral analytics can identify coaching patterns.

Learning platforms can monitor skill development.

Predictive models can detect declining engagement before it affects performance.

However, one element remains beyond the capability of any algorithm.

Recognizing leadership potential requires human judgment.

Leadership is not simply measured through outcomes.

It is observed through behavior, integrity, resilience, curiosity, and the ability to inspire others during uncertainty.

For this reason, I believe Artificial Intelligence should become an advisor in leadership development—not its decision maker.

Technology can identify patterns.

Leaders recognize people.

Organizations succeed when both capabilities work together.

Leadership Reflection

Some of the most successful leaders I have worked with were not the highest individual performers.

They were the people who consistently helped others become successful.

Leadership is measured not only by the results we produce ourselves, but by the leaders we develop for the future.

6.4 The AI Leadership Coaching Cycle

Within the KACL Framework, leadership coaching follows a continuous learning cycle.

Stage 1 – Observe

Operational data are collected from CRM systems, sales dashboards, coaching records, learning platforms, customer engagement metrics, and organizational performance indicators.

Stage 2 – Interpret

Artificial Intelligence identifies trends, compares behavioral patterns with historical organizational outcomes, and highlights areas where leadership interventions may produce the greatest impact.

Instead of generating generic recommendations, the system identifies context-specific developmental opportunities.

Stage 3 – Coach

The Field Force Manager reviews AI-generated observations together with personal field experience.

The coaching discussion therefore focuses not on explaining historical performance but on improving future leadership behaviors.

Coaching becomes evidence-informed, with less dependence on intuition alone.

Stage 4 - Measure

Subsequent organizational data determine whether coaching interventions produced measurable improvements.

Leadership development becomes a continuous feedback loop rather than an isolated annual activity.

FIGURE 10

THE DATA–INSIGHT–IMPACT CYCLE

Turning operational data into leadership improvement and organizational performance through continuous learning.

FIGURE NOTE: This cycle demonstrates how data and AI create a continuous feedback loop that strengthens leadership and drives organizational performance.

Source: Author's conceptual framework (KACL™).

6.5 Case Study – Coaching a Regional Manager

Consider a Regional Manager responsible for eight Medical Representatives.

Sales performance appears stable.

Traditional reporting suggests no immediate concern.

However, AI identifies several subtle changes over the previous eight weeks:

- Coaching frequency has decreased by 27%.
- One-to-one meetings are becoming shorter.
- CRM notes contain less qualitative insight.
- Follow-up actions after field visits have declined.
- Two experienced representatives have shown reduced customer engagement.
- Forecast accuracy has deteriorated.

None of these indicators alone would necessarily justify intervention.

Taken together, however, they suggest a decline in leadership effectiveness.

The AI platform recommends:

- an in-depth coaching session;
- observation of field coaching behaviors;
- review of delegation practices;
- reinforcement of coaching routines;
- follow-up assessment after thirty days.

The Field Force Manager evaluates these recommendations alongside contextual information and determines the most appropriate intervention.

The final decision remains human.

Artificial Intelligence accelerates diagnosis; it does not replace leadership judgment.

This approach is consistent with McKinsey's description of AI-enabled sales coaching, where managers transition from "performance inspectors" to "performance coaches." AI analyzes interactions at scale and surfaces high-impact coaching opportunities, allowing managers to spend more time developing people rather than reviewing reports.

6.6 Author's Insight

Throughout my leadership career, I gradually discovered that the quality of a Field Force Manager is reflected not by the number of reports reviewed but by the number of leaders successfully developed.

Commercial success rarely depends upon one exceptional manager.

It depends upon creating many capable managers.

Artificial Intelligence enables leaders to identify coaching opportunities earlier, monitor developmental progress more objectively, and allocate coaching time where it creates the greatest organizational value.

Technology cannot coach.

Leaders coach.

Artificial Intelligence simply helps leaders coach better.

THE AI-DRIVEN FIELD FORCE OPERATING SYSTEM™ (FFOS[2])

A New Operating System for Pharmaceutical Commercial Organizations

---

7.1 Why Pharmaceutical Organizations Need an Operating System

Most pharmaceutical companies possess well-developed organizational structures (Drucker, 2007).

They define reporting relationships.

They establish responsibilities.

They develop annual business plans.

They implement CRM systems.

They monitor commercial KPIs.

Yet despite these organizational capabilities, many companies continue to struggle with one persistent challenge:

Information moves much slower than business changes.

Commercial organizations often generate extraordinary volumes of information every day (Davenport & Harris, 2007).

Medical Representatives collect physician insights.

Regional Managers conduct coaching observations.

Marketing teams launch campaigns.

Medical Affairs develops scientific materials.

Market Access teams negotiate reimbursement.

Finance monitors commercial performance.

Business Intelligence generates dashboards.

Customer Relationship Management systems continuously record interactions.

---

[2] The Field Force Operating System™ (FFOS™) is an original conceptual operating model developed by the author to support AI-enabled commercial execution, leadership development, territory management, and organizational learning. The model represents the operational implementation component of the KACL Framework™.

Paradoxically, although more information exists than ever before, commercial decisions frequently remain slower than market dynamics.

The limitation is no longer information (Davenport & Harris, 2007).

The limitation is organizational coordination (Mintzberg, 1973).

McKinsey recently emphasized that organizations achieving sustainable AI advantage are redesigning operating models around faster decision-making, simplified workflows, and intelligent coordination instead of merely deploying additional digital tools.

The next evolution therefore requires something beyond another dashboard.

It requires an operating system.

7.2 Defining the Field Force Operating System (FFOS)

Within this book, the **Field Force Operating System (FFOS)** is proposed as a conceptual operating layer that connects commercial leadership, organizational intelligence, and Artificial Intelligence into a continuous decision-making ecosystem.

Unlike conventional CRM platforms, which primarily capture interactions, or Business Intelligence systems, which summarize historical performance, FFOS is designed to orchestrate how information flows, how decisions are supported, and how organizational learning is continuously reinforced (Payne & Frow, 2005; Davenport & Harris, 2007).

The purpose of FFOS is not to replace existing commercial systems.

Rather, it provides a conceptual framework through which those systems operate as an integrated leadership environment.

Under this approach:

- CRM systems become the primary source of customer interaction data.
- Commercial analytics platforms generate predictive insights.
- AI engines evaluate patterns and recommend actions.
- Managers provide contextual judgment, ethical oversight, and strategic direction.

- Organizational learning feeds back into the system to improve future decision-making.

The operating system therefore connects technology, people, and commercial processes into a unified decision architecture.

7.3 The Five Layers of FFOS

The proposed Field Force Operating System consists of five interconnected layers.

Layer 1 — Commercial Intelligence

This foundational layer captures commercial information from multiple enterprise systems, including CRM platforms, omnichannel engagement tools, sales reporting systems, market access data, learning platforms, and customer feedback mechanisms (Davenport & Harris, 2007).

Its primary purpose is to establish a unified and continuously updated source of commercial information.

Layer 2 — Predictive Intelligence

The second layer applies AI models to identify patterns, estimate probabilities, forecast commercial outcomes, detect emerging risks, and prioritize opportunities (Russell & Norvig, 2021).

Instead of reporting what has already occurred, this layer estimates what is most likely to occur if no managerial intervention is implemented.

Layer 3 — Leadership Intelligence

Technology alone cannot determine commercial priorities.

Leadership Intelligence represents the point at which managerial judgment, organizational experience, ethical considerations, and strategic objectives are integrated with AI-generated recommendations.

Within FFOS, this layer preserves human accountability while increasing decision quality.

Layer 4 — Organizational Execution

Once leadership decisions have been made, execution occurs across the commercial organization.

Regional Managers coach teams.

Medical Representatives engage healthcare professionals.

Marketing adjusts campaigns.

Medical Affairs supports scientific communication.

Supply Chain aligns product availability.

The operating system continuously monitors execution quality and organizational responsiveness (Kotter, 2012).

Layer 5 — Continuous Organizational Learning

Every commercial activity generates new organizational knowledge (Argyris & Schön, 1978; Senge, 2006).

Performance outcomes, coaching effectiveness, physician engagement patterns, forecast accuracy, and commercial execution quality are continuously reintroduced into the operating system.

Consequently, FFOS becomes progressively more effective over time.

Learning becomes an organizational capability, not only an individual one (Senge, 2006).

FIGURE 11

THE FIELD FORCE OPERATING SYSTEM™ (FFOS™)

An integrated intelligence-to-execution system that drives sustainable commercial performance through continuous learning.

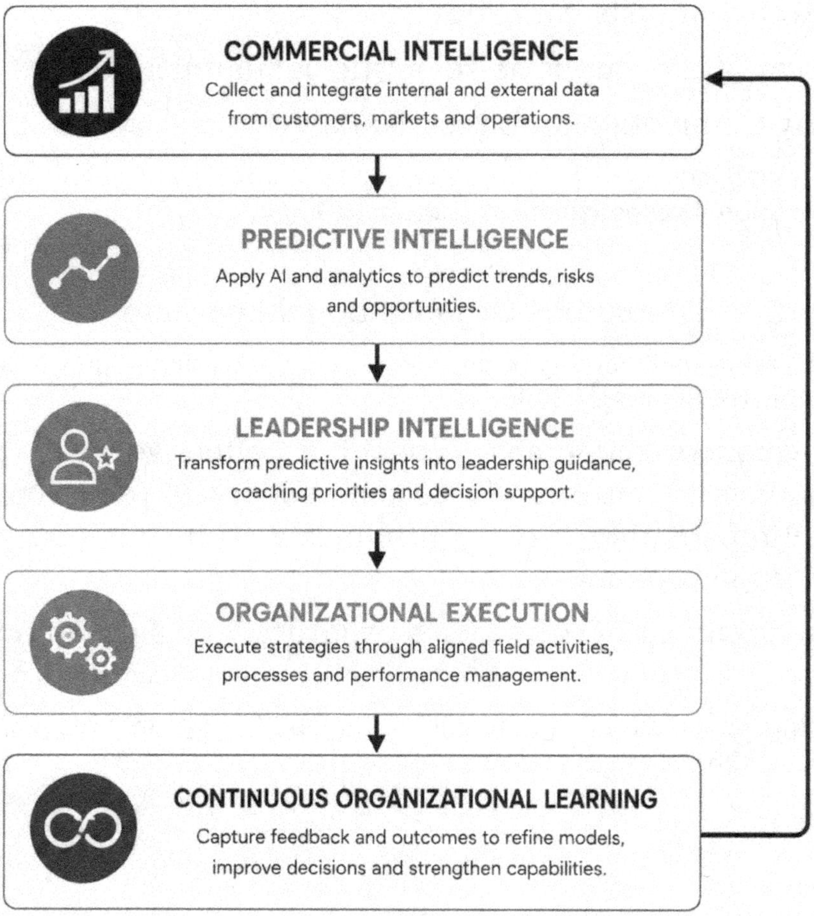

FIGURE NOTE: FFOS™ connects intelligence, leadership and execution in a closed-loop system that adapts and improves over time.

Source: Author's conceptual framework (KACL™).

Why the Future of Pharmaceutical Leadership Depends on Better Decisions Rather Than More Data

8.1 The Data Paradox

One of the greatest misconceptions surrounding digital transformation is the belief that organizations fail because they lack information (Davenport & Harris, 2007).

The opposite is increasingly true.

Modern pharmaceutical organizations generate unprecedented quantities of commercial information (Davenport & Harris, 2007).

Every physician interaction.

Every CRM activity.

Every digital campaign.

Every learning module.

Every coaching session.

Every customer engagement.

Every reimbursement update.

Every sales report.

Every forecasting cycle.

contributes additional data to the commercial ecosystem.

Paradoxically, despite this abundance of information, commercial leaders often report increasing uncertainty rather than greater confidence.

The challenge is no longer collecting information (Davenport & Harris, 2007).

The challenge is determining which information deserves managerial attention (Kahneman, 2011).

This phenomenon may be described as the Commercial Data Paradox.

The more information organizations generate, the more difficult it becomes for leaders to distinguish meaningful signals from operational noise.

According to Gartner, organizations are rapidly moving beyond Business Intelligence toward Decision Intelligence, an approach that combines data science, artificial intelligence, behavioral science, and managerial judgment to improve business decision-making. Gartner argues that organizations capable of operationalizing Decision Intelligence are better positioned to improve both the speed and quality of strategic decisions. (Gartner, 2024a)

Within pharmaceutical commercial organizations, this transition has profound implications.

Commercial leaders no longer require additional dashboards (Gartner, 2024a).

They require greater decision clarity (Davenport & Harris, 2007).

8.2 Decision Intelligence Versus Business Intelligence

Business Intelligence answers one question:

What happened?

Decision Intelligence asks four additional questions.

Why did it happen?

What is likely to happen next?

What should we do?

What will probably happen if we choose Option A instead of Option B?

This seemingly simple evolution fundamentally transforms commercial leadership (Davenport & Harris, 2007).

Traditional reporting systems primarily support observation (Davenport & Harris, 2007).

Decision Intelligence supports judgment (Gartner, 2024a).

Within pharmaceutical organizations, this distinction affects virtually every strategic activity, including:

- territory alignment;
- sales forecasting;
- coaching priorities;
- physician engagement;
- promotional investment;

- resource allocation;
- leadership succession planning.

FIGURE 12

EVOLUTION OF COMMERCIAL INTELLIGENCE

The progressive transformation of data into leadership excellence through increasing levels of intelligence and impact.

1 **OPERATIONAL DATA**
Raw data collected from systems, processes, customers and the market.

↓

2 **BUSINESS INTELLIGENCE**
Data is organized and analyzed to understand what has happened and why.

↓

3 **PREDICTIVE ANALYTICS**
Advanced analytics predict what is likely to happen and identify opportunities and risks.

↓

4 **ARTIFICIAL INTELLIGENCE**
AI algorithms learn from data, recognize patterns and generate recommendations.

↓

5 **DECISION INTELLIGENCE**
AI-powered insights are contextualized to support better, faster and more confident decisions.

↓

6 **LEADERSHIP EXCELLENCE**
Superior decisions drive stronger execution, engagement and sustainable results.

FIGURE NOTE: This evolution transforms raw data into leadership impact, enabling organizations to create sustainable competitive advantage.

Source: Author's conceptual framework (KACL™).

EXECUTIVE CASE STUDY

When the Organization Outgrew Its Management System

One of the most valuable leadership lessons I learned did not emerge from a successful commercial initiative.

It emerged during a period of rapid organizational growth.

As the commercial organization expanded, new territories were created, additional Regional Managers joined the organization, reporting structures became more sophisticated, and performance indicators continued to increase.

Initially, these developments appeared entirely positive.

More managers.

More reports.

More performance metrics.

More meetings.

More visibility.

At least, that was what we believed.

Gradually, however, an unexpected pattern began to emerge.

Managers were spending more time reviewing information than developing people.

Weekly meetings became increasingly focused on explaining historical reports rather than discussing future actions.

Field coaching sessions became less frequent.

Decision-making slowed.

Although the organization possessed more commercial information than ever before, leadership effectiveness did not improve at the same pace.

Looking back, I realized that the organization had quietly reached a turning point.

The commercial organization had evolved.

The management system had not.

We had expanded the business without redesigning how leadership operated.

The experience fundamentally changed the questions I asked as a leader.

Instead of asking,

"How can we generate more reports?"

I began asking,

"Which information actually changes leadership decisions?"

That distinction proved transformational.

Some reports disappeared.

Meetings became shorter.

Leadership conversations became more focused.

Managers recovered time for coaching, planning, and organizational development.

The experience ultimately shaped one of the central ideas presented throughout this book.

Organizational complexity cannot be managed simply by increasing information.

It requires improving decision quality.

Artificial Intelligence provides exactly this opportunity.

Instead of overwhelming managers with additional dashboards, AI can identify meaningful patterns, prioritize emerging risks, and highlight where leadership attention creates the greatest organizational value.

Technology should not increase complexity.

It should reduce it.

Leadership should not become more administrative as organizations grow.

It should become more strategic.

Leadership Reflection

Growth creates complexity (Mintzberg, 1973).

Complexity demands better management systems (Senge, 2006).

Artificial Intelligence should not replace leadership.

It should protect leaders from being consumed by complexity, allowing them to spend more time developing people and less time interpreting reports (McKinsey & Company, 2025a).

8.3 The Three Levels of Decision Making

The KACL Framework proposes that pharmaceutical commercial organizations make decisions across three interconnected levels.

Level One

Operational Decisions

Examples include:

- daily physician visits;
- territory routing;
- scheduling;
- promotional execution.

These decisions should increasingly become AI-assisted (Russell & Norvig, 2021).

Level Two

Managerial Decisions

Examples include:

- coaching priorities;
- territory restructuring;
- resource allocation;
- Regional Manager development.

These decisions require both predictive intelligence and experienced managerial judgment (Davenport & Harris, 2007).

Level Three

Strategic Decisions

Examples include:

- organizational redesign;
- commercial strategy;
- market expansion;
- leadership succession;
- long-term capability building.

Artificial Intelligence informs these decisions (Russell & Norvig, 2021).

Leadership owns them.

EXECUTIVE CASE STUDY

Strategic Planning Under Uncertainty

Throughout my leadership career, I came to realize that annual commercial planning was never simply an exercise in setting sales targets.

It was an exercise in making decisions under uncertainty.

Each planning cycle required balancing ambitious commercial objectives with limited organizational resources. Sales forecasts had to be translated into territory structures, workforce capacity, coaching priorities, incentive systems, training investments, and operational budgets.

Every decision influenced several others.

Increasing headcount affected coaching capacity.

Changing territory boundaries influenced customer relationships.

Adjusting incentive systems altered field behavior.

No decision existed in isolation.

One of the most difficult aspects of strategic planning was that nearly every important decision had to be made before complete information was available.

Market conditions changed.

Competitive activities evolved.

Healthcare regulations shifted.

Customer expectations developed continuously.

Despite this uncertainty, leadership could not postpone decisions.

Planning required moving forward with imperfect information while remaining prepared to adapt as new evidence emerged.

Over time, I learned that successful planning depended less on producing accurate forecasts and more on building organizations capable of responding quickly when assumptions changed.

This perspective fundamentally changed my understanding of commercial leadership.

The objective was not to predict the future perfectly.

The objective was to prepare the organization for multiple possible futures.

Artificial Intelligence significantly strengthens this capability.

Instead of relying exclusively on historical reports, AI can continuously evaluate market signals, detect emerging commercial trends, simulate alternative planning scenarios, and identify risks before they become visible through traditional performance indicators.

Yet even with advanced predictive analytics, leadership remains responsible for making the final strategic choices.

Planning is not only a mathematical exercise.

It requires judgment, experience, organizational awareness, and an understanding of people.

Technology improves forecasts.

Leadership determines direction.

Leadership Reflection

One lesson has consistently guided my approach to strategic planning.

Organizations rarely fail because their forecasts were imperfect (Kotter, 2012).

They fail because they become unwilling to adapt after reality changes.

The strongest commercial organizations are not those that predict the future most accurately (Taleb, 2007).

They are the ones that adjust to change the fastest.

Author's Insight

During my years managing pharmaceutical field organizations, I realized that leadership quality could often be measured by a single characteristic:

the ability to make good decisions under uncertainty.

Information alone never guaranteed success (Drucker, 2007).

Experience alone never guaranteed success (Mintzberg, 1973).

Artificial Intelligence alone will never guarantee success (Russell & Norvig, 2021).

Sustainable commercial excellence emerges when experienced leaders consistently make better decisions using better information, supported by intelligent analytical systems (Davenport & Harris, 2007).

This, in my opinion, represents the future of pharmaceutical leadership.

BUILDING A SELF-LEARNING COMMERCIAL ORGANIZATION

Transforming Pharmaceutical Field Organizations into Continuous Learning Systems

9.1 The Next Evolution of Commercial Organizations

For decades, pharmaceutical companies have invested heavily in recruiting talented Medical Representatives, developing experienced Regional Managers, implementing Customer Relationship Management (CRM) systems, and establishing standardized commercial processes (Zoltners et al., 2009; Payne & Frow, 2005).

These investments have undoubtedly improved commercial performance (Zoltners et al., 2009).

However, one critical limitation remains.

Most commercial organizations continue to learn episodically rather than continuously (Senge, 2006).

Knowledge is generated every day across the field organization, yet much of that knowledge remains localized within individual territories, Regional Managers, or business units. Valuable commercial insights are frequently discussed during coaching sessions, regional meetings, or quarterly business reviews but are rarely transformed into institutional knowledge that benefits the entire organization (Argyris & Schön, 1978).

This represents a significant organizational inefficiency (Senge, 2006).

In knowledge-intensive industries such as pharmaceuticals, competitive advantage increasingly depends not only on acquiring information but also on converting experience into organizational capability (Barney, 1991; Senge, 2006).

Artificial Intelligence introduces an opportunity to fundamentally redesign how pharmaceutical organizations learn (Russell & Norvig, 2021).

Instead of relying primarily on periodic reviews and retrospective reporting, organizations can establish continuous learning systems in which every commercial interaction contributes to future organizational intelligence (Davenport & Harris, 2007; Senge, 2006).

9.2 From Individual Experience to Organizational Intelligence

Traditional commercial organizations often depend upon the experience of exceptional individuals (Drucker, 2007).

A highly successful Regional Manager develops effective coaching techniques.

An experienced Medical Representative discovers an effective physician engagement strategy.

A Field Force Manager identifies a successful territory planning approach.

Unfortunately, these practices frequently remain isolated (Argyris & Schön, 1978).

When experienced employees leave the organization, valuable knowledge often leaves with them (Nonaka & Takeuchi, 1995).

Artificial Intelligence provides an opportunity to reduce this dependency on individual memory (Russell & Norvig, 2021).

By continuously analyzing commercial interactions, coaching practices, customer engagement patterns, forecasting accuracy, and organizational outcomes, AI can help convert individual expertise into repeatable organizational knowledge (Davenport & Harris, 2007; Nonaka & Takeuchi, 1995).

This transition represents one of the defining characteristics of what this book describes as a **Self-Learning Commercial Organization**.

Instead of asking employees to remember best practices, the organization itself becomes capable of identifying, preserving, and continuously improving them (Senge, 2006).

Gartner's research on adaptive learning similarly argues that organizations should move away from one-size-fits-all learning models toward personalized, continuously evolving learning journeys supported by AI (Gartner, 2024b).

EXECUTIVE CASE STUDY

Leading Cross-Functional Organizations

One of the most significant changes in my leadership philosophy occurred when I realized that commercial performance is rarely determined by the commercial department alone.

Early in my management career, I believed that improving sales execution depended primarily on strengthening field force performance.

Experience gradually demonstrated a much broader reality.

Commercial success is the outcome of multiple organizational functions working toward the same objective.

During several large-scale commercial initiatives, I worked closely with professionals from medical affairs, marketing, finance, human resources, regulatory affairs, supply chain, training, and business operations.

Each function contributed unique expertise.

Medical teams ensured scientific accuracy.

Marketing developed communication strategies.

Finance evaluated commercial investments.

Human resources supported organizational capability.

Training departments prepared field teams.

Supply chain maintained product availability.

Viewed independently, each function appeared successful.

The real leadership challenge was ensuring that all functions moved in the same direction at the same time.

Cross-functional leadership required far more than coordination.

It required building trust between departments with different priorities, different performance indicators, and sometimes different perspectives on success.

Many organizational delays were not caused by a lack of competence.

They resulted from different teams making individually correct decisions that were not organizationally aligned.

This experience fundamentally changed my understanding of leadership.

The role of senior leadership is not to manage every department.

It is to create alignment between departments.

Artificial Intelligence can significantly improve cross-functional visibility.

Shared dashboards, predictive analytics, workflow monitoring, and integrated planning systems allow leaders to recognize emerging organizational bottlenecks much earlier than traditional reporting methods.

However, technology alone cannot create collaboration.

Departments cooperate because leaders establish common objectives, encourage mutual trust, and reinforce a shared organizational purpose.

AI strengthens coordination.

Leadership creates alignment.

Long-term commercial excellence requires both.

Leadership Reflection

Organizations rarely succeed because every department performs perfectly (Senge, 2006).

They succeed because different departments understand how their individual contributions support a common objective (Kotter, 2012).

The most valuable leadership capability is not controlling functions.

It is connecting them (Mintzberg, 1973).

9.3 The Commercial Learning Cycle

Within the KACL Framework, organizational learning follows five interconnected stages.

Stage 1 — Experience

Commercial activities generate continuous operational information (Davenport & Harris, 2007).

Examples include:

- physician interactions;
- coaching sessions;
- sales forecasts;
- CRM documentation;
- omnichannel engagement;
- commercial negotiations;

- market observations.

Every interaction becomes a potential learning opportunity (Argyris & Schön, 1978).

Stage 2 — Knowledge Capture

Instead of allowing valuable experience to remain isolated, the organization systematically captures operational knowledge through integrated commercial systems (Nonaka & Takeuchi, 1995).

Customer feedback.

Coaching observations.

Performance indicators.

Digital engagement.

Training outcomes.

Forecast deviations.

All become structured organizational assets (Senge, 2006).

Stage 3 — AI Interpretation

Artificial Intelligence evaluates relationships across thousands of commercial events (Russell & Norvig, 2021).

Instead of merely identifying statistical correlations, AI detects behavioral patterns associated with successful commercial outcomes (Davenport & Harris, 2007).

Examples include:

- coaching behaviors consistently associated with higher team performance;
- physician engagement strategies producing stronger long-term relationships;
- territory structures generating sustainable growth;
- learning activities associated with faster employee development.

This transforms raw operational information into actionable organizational intelligence (Davenport & Harris, 2007; Senge, 2006).

Stage 4 — Leadership Integration

Artificial Intelligence does not determine organizational policy (OECD, 2024).

Commercial leaders evaluate AI-generated insights within the broader strategic, ethical, scientific, and commercial context (World Health Organization, 2021; OECD, 2024).

Leadership remains responsible for:

- organizational priorities;
- change management;
- talent development;
- compliance;
- strategic direction.

Technology informs.

Leadership decides.

Stage 5 — Organizational Adaptation

Validated improvements become integrated into commercial operations (Senge, 2006).

Training programs evolve.

Coaching standards improve.

Territory strategies adapt.

Leadership practices mature.

Consequently, the organization itself becomes progressively more capable over time.

Learning no longer depends solely upon individual experience (Nonaka & Takeuchi, 1995).

It becomes an institutional capability (Barney, 1991).

FIGURE 13

THE SELF-LEARNING COMMERCIAL ORGANIZATION

A continuous cycle where experience is transformed into better decisions, adapted strategies and superior commercial performance.

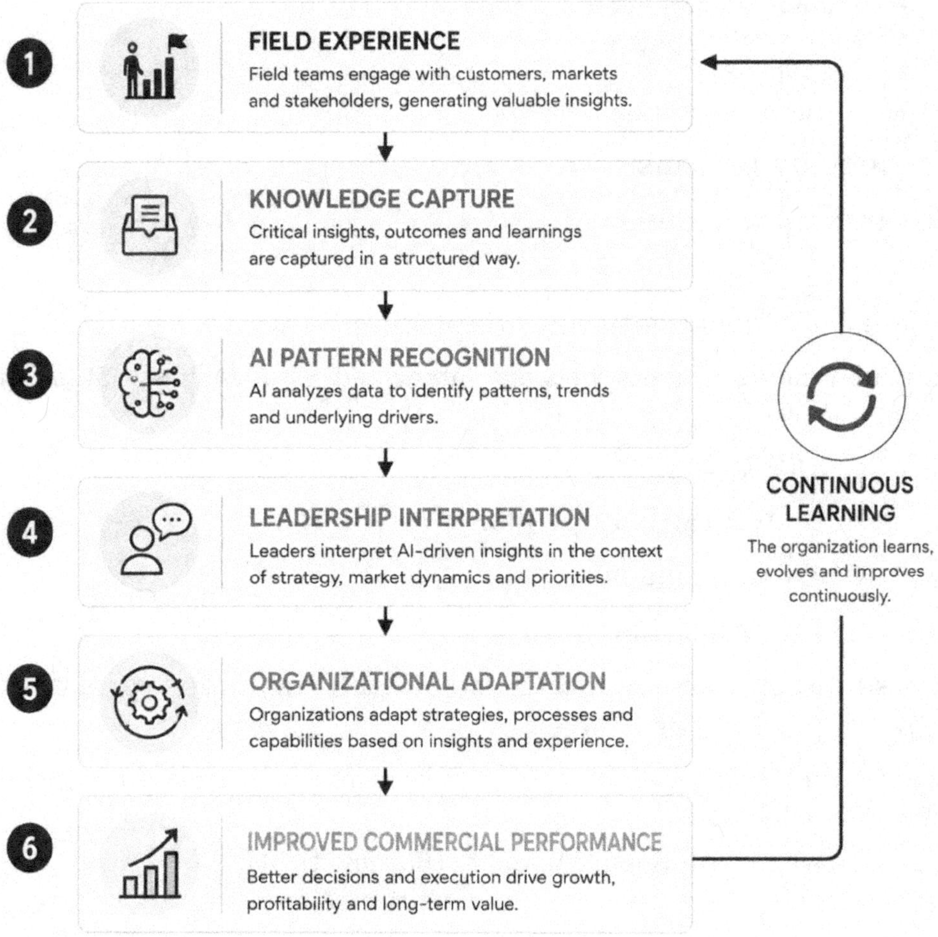

FIGURE NOTE: A self-learning organization turns field experience into organizational intelligence, enabling continuous adaptation and sustainable competitive advantage.

Source: Author's conceptual framework (KACL™).

9.4 Why This Matters for Pharmaceutical Companies

Unlike many industries, pharmaceutical organizations operate under conditions where scientific knowledge, customer expectations, regulatory requirements, and competitive dynamics evolve continuously (IQVIA, 2024).

Consequently, commercial organizations that learn slowly gradually lose competitive relevance (Senge, 2006).

Organizations capable of learning continuously gain cumulative advantages over time (Barney, 1991; Senge, 2006).

McKinsey argues that organizations creating lasting value from generative AI redesign workflows and organizational processes instead of simply automating existing tasks. In parallel, Gartner emphasizes that faster decision-making, adaptive learning, and AI-supported enablement improve organizational agility and commercial performance (McKinsey & Company, 2025a; Gartner, 2024a, 2024b, 2024c).

Within pharmaceutical organizations, this means AI should not simply improve productivity (McKinsey & Company, 2025a).

It should improve organizational learning (Senge, 2006).

Author's Insight

During my years managing pharmaceutical organizations across multiple regions, I observed that every successful team possessed valuable knowledge.

The problem was never the absence of expertise.

The problem was that organizational learning depended too heavily on individuals (Nonaka & Takeuchi, 1995).

When experienced managers changed roles or left the company, much of that knowledge disappeared with them.

In my opinion, Artificial Intelligence provides an opportunity to fundamentally change this pattern.

The future competitive advantage of pharmaceutical organizations will not depend solely upon having talented employees (Barney, 1991).

It will depend upon building organizations that continuously learn from those employees.

Proposed Contribution

One of the principal contributions of this book is the proposition that Artificial Intelligence should be viewed not merely as an automation technology but as an organizational learning capability.

Within the proposed KACL Framework, AI supports three interconnected objectives:

1. Improving managerial decisions.

2. Strengthening leadership capability.
3. Transforming organizational learning into a continuous strategic asset.

This perspective extends beyond conventional discussions of AI implementation, which often focus primarily on productivity gains or cost reduction (Brynjolfsson & McAfee, 2014; McKinsey & Company, 2025a).

IMPLEMENTING AI-DRIVEN COMMERCIAL TRANSFORMATION

From Vision to Execution

10.1 Why AI Projects Fail

Artificial Intelligence has become one of the most significant strategic priorities across the pharmaceutical industry (McKinsey & Company, 2025; IQVIA, 2024). Yet despite substantial investments in AI technologies, many organizations continue to struggle to generate measurable business value (McKinsey & Company, 2025a).

The challenge is rarely the technology itself (Davenport & Harris, 2007).

Instead, implementation failures frequently result from organizational factors including fragmented governance, unclear strategic priorities, inadequate leadership engagement, insufficient change management, and poor integration into existing business workflows (Deloitte, 2024; Kotter, 2012).

McKinsey's research consistently emphasizes that organizations creating measurable value from AI redesign workflows, simplify operating models, and embed AI into everyday business decisions instead of treating it as a stand-alone technology initiative.

Similarly, Gartner argues that organizations improve commercial growth when they accelerate decision-making, build adaptability, and integrate AI into operational leadership instead of limiting AI to analytical functions.

Within pharmaceutical commercial organizations, this distinction is particularly important (IQVIA, 2024).

The objective is not implementing Artificial Intelligence.

The objective is improving commercial leadership.

10.2 The Four Phases of Commercial AI Transformation

The KACL Framework proposes that successful AI implementation should follow four progressive organizational phases.

Instead of attempting enterprise-wide transformation immediately, organizations should gradually increase AI maturity while strengthening leadership capability (Kotter, 2012).

Phase I — Digital Foundation

The first phase focuses on establishing reliable commercial data and standardized operational processes (Davenport & Harris, 2007).

Core objectives include:

- CRM data quality
- standardized physician segmentation
- consistent KPI definitions
- integrated commercial reporting
- digital adoption by field teams
- governance of commercial information

Without trusted data, Artificial Intelligence cannot generate trusted recommendations (Russell & Norvig, 2021).

At this stage, leadership should prioritize organizational discipline rather than technological sophistication (Drucker, 2007).

Phase II — Decision Intelligence

Once commercial information becomes reliable, organizations begin using predictive analytics to support managerial decisions (Davenport & Harris, 2007).

Examples include:

- sales forecasting;
- territory optimization;
- physician prioritization;
- coaching recommendations;
- commercial risk identification.

Importantly, AI supports decisions without replacing managerial responsibility (Russell & Norvig, 2021).

Leaders remain accountable for evaluating recommendations within scientific, ethical, and commercial contexts (OECD, 2024; World Health Organization, 2021).

Phase III — Adaptive Leadership

The third phase represents a significant cultural transition (Kotter, 2012).

Managers no longer spend most of their time collecting information (Davenport & Harris, 2007).

Instead, they increasingly focus on:

- leadership development;

- organizational learning;
- cross-functional collaboration;
- strategic planning;
- coaching;
- continuous improvement.

Artificial Intelligence reduces analytical workload while expanding managerial capacity for leadership (McKinsey & Company, 2025a).

This transition aligns with Gartner's recommendation that AI should increase the **span of value** of managers—not simply their span of control. Managers spend less time reviewing reports and more time developing people, supporting change, and improving strategic execution.

Phase IV — Autonomous Organizational Learning

The final phase does not imply autonomous leadership.

Rather, it describes organizations capable of continuously improving through integrated learning systems (Senge, 2006).

Commercial data,

AI interpretation,

leadership decisions,

organizational execution,

and performance outcomes

become part of a continuous improvement cycle.

Within this environment, AI evolves from a decision-support tool into an organizational learning capability (Davenport & Harris, 2007; Senge, 2006).

The organization becomes increasingly adaptive without reducing human accountability (OECD, 2024).

FIGURE 14

COMMERCIAL AI TRANSFORMATION ROADMAP

A phased journey from building the foundation to becoming a self-learning, adaptive and high-performing commercial organization.

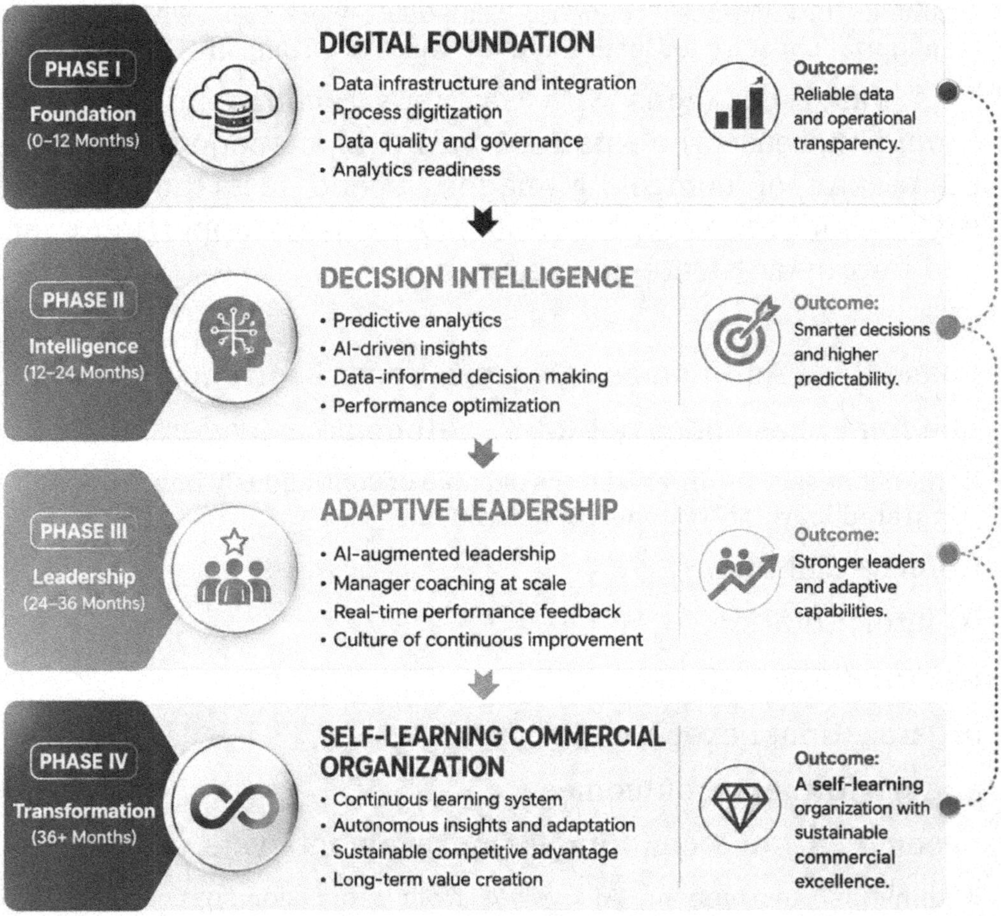

FIGURE NOTE: This roadmap provides a structured path for commercial organizations to integrate AI and build future-ready capabilities step by step.

Source: Author's conceptual framework (KACL™).

10.3 Leadership Responsibilities During AI Transformation

Technology implementation alone does not create transformation (Kotter, 2012).

Leadership determines whether AI becomes a competitive advantage or an underutilized investment (Barney, 1991).

Within the KACL Framework, Field Force Managers and Commercial Directors assume five primary responsibilities during transformation:

Strategic Alignment

Ensure AI initiatives support commercial strategy instead of becoming isolated technology projects.

Organizational Trust

Build confidence by explaining how AI supports—not replaces—employees.

Transparent communication reduces resistance and increases adoption.

Capability Development

Invest in data literacy, analytical thinking, coaching skills, and digital leadership.

Organizations should develop leaders capable of working effectively alongside AI rather than competing with it (Brynjolfsson & McAfee, 2014).

Governance

Establish clear accountability for AI-assisted decisions.

Ethical oversight, regulatory compliance, explainability, and human review remain essential within healthcare organizations. Lessons from AI governance programs in large biopharmaceutical companies show that effective AI deployment depends on embedding governance into existing business processes, focusing on risk management, and continuously educating employees (Mökander et al., 2024).

Continuous Evaluation

Commercial transformation should be evaluated using measurable business outcomes rather than technology adoption metrics alone (McKinsey & Company, 2025a).

Examples include:

- coaching quality;
- forecast accuracy;
- decision speed;
- physician engagement;
- commercial productivity;
- employee development.

10.4 Common Implementation Mistakes

Analysis of industry practice suggests several recurring implementation errors: (McKinsey & Company, 2025; Gartner, 2025).

Technology-first thinking

Organizations purchase AI tools before defining leadership problems.

Poor-quality commercial data

AI recommendations are only as reliable as the information on which they are trained (Russell & Norvig, 2021).

Insufficient leadership engagement

AI initiatives delegated exclusively to IT departments rarely transform commercial decision-making (Kotter, 2012).

Ignoring organizational change

Successful transformation depends on changing behaviors, not only deploying software (Kotter, 2012).

Overestimating automation

Organizations sometimes expect AI to replace managerial judgment rather than strengthen it.

These patterns are consistent with McKinsey's observation that scaling AI requires redesigning workflows and operating models —not merely adding new technology.

Case Study (Illustrative)

A multinational pharmaceutical company introduces AI-assisted forecasting across its national sales organization.

Initially, Regional Managers resist the system because they perceive it as replacing their experience.

The Commercial Director reframes the initiative.

Instead of presenting AI as a forecasting engine, leadership positions it as a **decision-support partner** designed to improve coaching conversations and territory planning.

Within six months:

- Forecast discussions become evidence-based.
- Coaching sessions focus on future opportunities rather than historical explanations.
- Regional Managers begin requesting additional AI insights rather than resisting them.
- Cross-functional planning becomes faster because all departments work from a common analytical foundation.

The technology did not transform the organization by itself.

Leadership did.

Author's Insight

During my career, I learned that transformation rarely fails because organizations choose the wrong technology.

More often, transformation fails because leaders underestimate the importance of people.

Employees do not resist Artificial Intelligence (Kotter, 2012).

They resist uncertainty.

When leaders communicate purpose clearly, involve managers early, and demonstrate how AI strengthens rather than diminishes professional expertise, adoption accelerates naturally.

Sustainable transformation therefore begins with leadership—not software.

11.1 Looking Beyond Artificial Intelligence

Throughout this book, Artificial Intelligence has been examined as an important enabler of commercial transformation. However, focusing exclusively on AI risks overlooking a more fundamental reality.

Technology itself does not create competitive advantage (Barney, 1991).

Organizations do.

The future pharmaceutical company will not be defined by the sophistication of its algorithms, the size of its data warehouse, or the number of AI applications deployed across commercial operations.

Instead, success will depend upon how effectively organizations integrate technology, leadership, organizational learning, ethical governance, and human capability into a coherent commercial system.

Artificial Intelligence will become increasingly invisible.

Leadership will become increasingly visible.

Just as Customer Relationship Management systems eventually became standard business infrastructure rather than strategic differentiators, Artificial Intelligence is likely to evolve into an expected organizational capability rather than a unique competitive advantage (McKinsey & Company, 2025c, 2026).

The organizations that distinguish themselves in 2035 will therefore not be those that simply possess AI (Brynjolfsson & McAfee, 2014).

They will be those that lead effectively with AI.

11.2 The Future Role of the Medical Representative

Predictions regarding the disappearance of Medical Representatives have appeared repeatedly over the past three decades (Zoltners et al., 2009).

Each wave of technological innovation—from CRM systems to digital detailing, virtual meetings, omnichannel engagement, and generative AI—has been accompanied by speculation that face-to-face commercial roles would gradually disappear.

Evidence suggests a different trajectory.

The role is evolving; it is not disappearing (IQVIA, 2024).

Routine promotional activities will continue to decline.

Conversely, the importance of scientific dialogue, clinical interpretation, relationship development, patient-centered communication, and complex stakeholder engagement will continue to increase.

Artificial Intelligence will increasingly support representatives by:

- recommending physician priorities;
- preparing personalized scientific summaries;
- suggesting follow-up strategies;
- identifying educational needs;
- forecasting engagement opportunities.

However, trust, empathy, credibility, and professional relationships will remain fundamentally human (Goleman et al., 2013).

Consequently, the Medical Representative of 2035 will function less as a product promoter and more as a scientific engagement consultant supported by intelligent decision systems.

11.3 The Future Regional Manager

The responsibilities of Regional Managers are likely to change more dramatically than those of Medical Representatives (Mintzberg, 1973).

Historically, Regional Managers devoted considerable time to reviewing reports, monitoring KPIs, evaluating sales performance, and preparing business reviews (Zoltners et al., 2009).

Many of these analytical activities will become increasingly automated (McKinsey & Company, 2025a).

Consequently, Regional Managers will spend proportionally more time on:

- leadership coaching;
- organizational development;
- change management;
- cross-functional collaboration;
- talent development;

- strategic planning.

Artificial Intelligence will continuously monitor commercial indicators.

Regional Managers will increasingly focus on developing people.

Leadership therefore becomes less administrative and more developmental (Heifetz et al., 2009).

11.4 The Future Field Force Manager

Within the KACL Framework, the Field Force Manager becomes the principal architect of organizational capability.

Instead of supervising sales performance alone, future Field Force Managers will coordinate:

- commercial intelligence;
- leadership development;
- AI governance;
- adaptive learning;
- cross-functional integration;
- organizational resilience.

The position evolves from operational management toward enterprise leadership (Drucker, 2007).

Field Force Managers become organizational designers rather than performance supervisors (Mintzberg, 1973).

FIGURE 15

EVOLUTION OF LEADERSHIP RESPONSIBILITIES

The shift from traditional operational roles to future-focused leadership responsibilities.

LEADERSHIP LEVEL	TRADITIONAL ORGANIZATION	→	FUTURE ORGANIZATION
MEDICAL REPRESENTATIVE	Product Promotion	→	Scientific Engagement Advisor
REGIONAL MANAGER	Sales Supervision	→	Leadership Coach
FIELD FORCE MANAGER	Performance Management	→	Organizational Architect
COMMERCIAL DIRECTOR	Commercial Strategy	→	Transformation Leader
GENERAL MANAGER	Business Operations	→	Enterprise Capability Builder

FIGURE NOTE: Leadership roles evolve from executing tasks to shaping systems, developing people and building sustainable commercial capabilities.

Source: Author's conceptual framework (KACL™).

11.5 The Future Pharmaceutical Organization

The pharmaceutical organization of 2035 will differ from today's organizations in several fundamental ways.

Information will no longer flow primarily upward through hierarchical reporting structures.

Instead, intelligence will circulate continuously across interconnected organizational networks.

Decision-making will become increasingly decentralized while remaining strategically aligned (Senge, 2006).

Commercial planning will evolve from annual exercises into continuously updated adaptive processes.

Leadership development will become data-informed and individualized (Gartner, 2025).

Cross-functional collaboration will replace departmental optimization.

Artificial Intelligence will provide predictive recommendations.

Human leaders will provide purpose, ethics, accountability, and strategic judgment.

Organizations will increasingly resemble adaptive ecosystems rather than traditional hierarchies (Senge, 2006).

11.6 The Human Advantage

Perhaps the greatest misconception surrounding Artificial Intelligence is the assumption that technological progress inevitably reduces the importance of people.

The opposite may prove true.

As analytical tasks become increasingly automated, uniquely human capabilities become more valuable (Goleman et al., 2013).

These include:

- ethical judgment;
- emotional intelligence;
- coaching;
- creativity;
- negotiation;
- organizational trust;
- cultural leadership;
- strategic vision.

Consequently, the future pharmaceutical organization will become simultaneously more technological and more human (Brynjolfsson & McAfee, 2014).

Technology will perform analysis (Kotter, 2012).

People will provide meaning.

FIGURE 16

THE HUMAN–AI PARTNERSHIP

AI provides intelligence and scale; leaders provide meaning and direction. Together, they create adaptive commercial excellence.

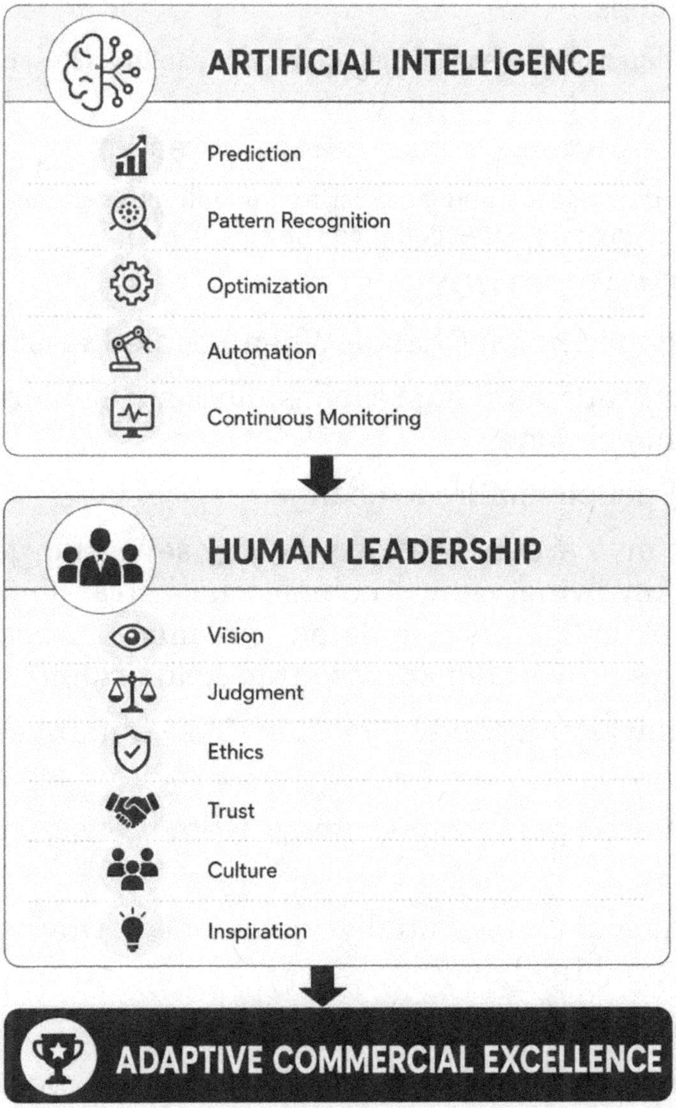

FIGURE NOTE: Sustainable excellence emerges when AI capabilities and human leadership are integrated in purpose.

Source: Author's conceptual framework (KACL™).

11.7 The Future Begins with Leadership

Many organizations continue asking an important question:

How should we implement Artificial Intelligence?

A more important question may be:

How should leadership evolve in order to fully benefit from Artificial Intelligence?

Technology alone does not create adaptive organizations (Kotter, 2012).

Leadership does.

Artificial Intelligence increases managerial capability (Russell & Norvig, 2021).

Leadership determines organizational direction.

Organizations that understand this distinction will likely define the future of pharmaceutical commercial excellence (Barney, 1991).

EXECUTIVE CASE STUDY

Leading Organizational Change When People Resist Change

One of the most demanding responsibilities of senior leadership is not creating change.

It is helping people embrace change.

Throughout my career, I participated in several organizational initiatives involving new commercial strategies, revised performance indicators, updated planning processes, and different ways of working across large field organizations.

From a technical perspective, most of these initiatives were well designed.

From a human perspective, they were considerably more difficult.

Many team members initially questioned why established methods needed to change.

Some managers preferred familiar routines.

Others worried that new performance measures would increase complexity rather than improve effectiveness.

Interestingly, resistance rarely resulted from disagreement with the strategic objective.

It resulted from uncertainty.

People generally support change once they understand its purpose, their role within it, and the expected benefits.

This experience gradually transformed my own leadership approach.

I learned that successful transformation begins long before implementation.

It begins with communication.

Before introducing new systems or performance expectations, leaders must explain why change is necessary, what problem it solves, and how success will be measured.

Equally important, leaders must create opportunities for people to ask questions, express concerns, and contribute ideas.

When employees participate in the transformation process, they become partners in change rather than passive recipients of it.

Artificial Intelligence can significantly improve organizational transformation.

AI can identify adoption patterns, monitor implementation progress, detect early signs of resistance, and provide leaders with real-time organizational insights.

However, technology cannot replace trust.

People rarely change because software tells them to.

They change because they trust the leaders guiding them through uncertainty.

Ultimately, I learned that transformation is not an operational project.

It is a leadership responsibility.

Technology accelerates change.

Leadership makes change sustainable.

Leadership Reflection

Organizations do not resist change.

People resist uncertainty (Kotter, 2012).

The responsibility of leadership is to replace uncertainty with understanding, confidence, and a shared sense of purpose (Heifetz et al., 2009).

When people understand why change matters, implementation becomes significantly easier.

Author's Insight

During my career, I had the opportunity to lead commercial organizations operating under very different market conditions, cultures, and healthcare systems.

Despite these differences, I consistently observed one principle.

Sustainable commercial success was never determined solely by products, market share, or organizational size.

It was determined by leadership quality.

Artificial Intelligence will undoubtedly transform pharmaceutical organizations.

Yet I believe its greatest contribution will not be technological.

It will be enabling leaders to spend less time managing information and more time developing people.

Ultimately, the future of pharmaceutical commercial excellence will belong to organizations that successfully combine intelligent technology with deeply human leadership.

Proposed Legacy Statement

The central proposition of this book may therefore be summarized in a single statement:

The future competitive advantage of pharmaceutical organizations will not be determined by Artificial Intelligence itself, but by the ability of commercial leaders to integrate Artificial Intelligence, organizational learning, ethical governance, and human leadership into a continuously adaptive commercial system.

This principle forms the conceptual foundation of the Kavun Adaptive Commercial Leadership Framework (KACL) and the Field Force Operating System (FFOS) proposed throughout this book.

THE NINE PRINCIPLES OF ADAPTIVE COMMERCIAL LEADERSHIP

A Leadership Manifesto for the AI Era

12.1 Beyond Artificial Intelligence

Throughout this book, Artificial Intelligence has been examined from multiple perspectives, including commercial operations, territory management, leadership development, organizational learning, predictive analytics, and commercial transformation (Davenport & Harris, 2007; Russell & Norvig, 2021).

However, the central argument of this book has never been that Artificial Intelligence itself represents the future of pharmaceutical organizations.

Rather, this book has consistently proposed that **leadership** remains the decisive factor.

Technology changes.

Markets evolve.

Healthcare systems transform.

Yet organizations ultimately succeed or fail according to the quality of leadership guiding those changes (Kotter, 2012).

Artificial Intelligence expands managerial capability (Russell & Norvig, 2021).

Leadership determines organizational direction (Drucker, 2007).

Consequently, the future of pharmaceutical commercial excellence depends not upon replacing human leaders, but upon enabling them to lead more effectively.

This philosophy forms the foundation of the following nine principles.

Principle One

Leadership Before Technology

Technology should never determine organizational strategy.

Leadership determines strategy.

Technology supports execution.

Organizations investing primarily in software while neglecting leadership capability are unlikely to achieve sustainable transformation (Kotter, 2012; McKinsey & Company, 2025a).

Artificial Intelligence should therefore be viewed as an organizational capability serving leadership without replacing it.

Principle Two

Decisions Before Data

Modern organizations rarely suffer from insufficient information (Davenport & Harris, 2007).

They suffer from excessive information.

Collecting more data does not automatically improve organizational performance.

Better decisions do.

Commercial intelligence should therefore be evaluated according to the quality of managerial decisions it enables rather than the quantity of reports it generates (Kahneman, 2011).

Principle Three

Coaching Before Controlling

The role of commercial leadership is evolving.

Managers should spend progressively less time supervising activities and increasingly more time developing people (Heifetz et al., 2009).

Artificial Intelligence can evaluate performance (Goleman et al., 2013).

Only leaders can develop potential.

The organizations of the future will therefore distinguish themselves through coaching excellence rather than administrative control.

Principle Four

Prediction Before Reaction

Traditional management reacts.

Adaptive leadership anticipates.

Artificial Intelligence enables organizations to recognize emerging commercial opportunities and organizational risks before they become visible through conventional reporting (Davenport & Harris, 2007; Russell & Norvig, 2021).

Competitive advantage increasingly depends upon acting earlier rather than working harder.

Principle Five

Organizational Learning Before Organizational Memory

Successful organizations do not merely accumulate experience.

They continuously transform experience into organizational capability (Nonaka & Takeuchi, 1995; Senge, 2006).

Every physician interaction.

Every coaching session.

Every commercial initiative.

Every strategic decision.

contributes to a continuously evolving organizational knowledge system.

Artificial Intelligence accelerates this learning process (Senge, 2006; Russell & Norvig, 2021).

Leadership institutionalizes it.

Principle Six

Ethics Before Automation

Healthcare organizations possess responsibilities extending beyond commercial performance (World Health Organization, 2021).

Patient welfare.

Scientific integrity.

Professional trust.

Regulatory compliance.

Ethical leadership therefore remains indispensable regardless of technological progress (OECD, 2024).

Artificial Intelligence may recommend actions. Human leaders remain accountable for their consequences (OECD, 2024; World Health Organization, 2021).

Principle Seven

Adaptation Before Standardization

The pharmaceutical environment changes continuously (IQVIA, 2024).

Organizations built upon rigid procedures gradually lose competitiveness.

Adaptive organizations continuously revise commercial strategies, leadership practices, territory structures, learning systems, and customer engagement models according to changing market conditions (Senge, 2006; Kotter, 2012).

Artificial Intelligence supports adaptation.

Leadership makes adaptation possible.

Principle Eight

Organizational Intelligence Before Individual Expertise

Exceptional employees create temporary advantage.

Exceptional organizations create sustainable advantage.

Commercial knowledge should therefore become institutional rather than individual (Nonaka & Takeuchi, 1995).

Organizations capable of continuously capturing, refining, and sharing knowledge outperform organizations dependent upon isolated expertise.

This principle forms one of the core foundations of the proposed Field Force Operating System.

Principle Nine

Human Leadership as the Ultimate Competitive Advantage

Throughout every technological revolution, predictions have emerged suggesting that technology would eventually replace leadership.

History has consistently demonstrated otherwise (Drucker, 2007).

Technology changes tools.

Leadership changes organizations.

Artificial Intelligence will continue transforming pharmaceutical commercial operations for decades to come.

Nevertheless, vision,

trust,

judgment,

ethics,

purpose,

inspiration,

and courage

remain uniquely human capabilities.

The organizations defining pharmaceutical commercial excellence in the coming decades will not necessarily possess the most sophisticated algorithms (Brynjolfsson & McAfee, 2014).

They will possess leaders most capable of integrating intelligent technology with deeply human leadership (Heifetz et al., 2009).

The KACL Declaration

The central proposition of this book may therefore be summarized as follows:

Artificial Intelligence should not be viewed as a replacement for pharmaceutical commercial leadership, but as an organizational capability that enhances leadership through better decisions, continuous learning, ethical governance, and adaptive execution. Sustainable competitive advantage will belong to organizations that successfully integrate human leadership, organizational intelligence, and Artificial Intelligence into a continuously evolving commercial system.

This proposition constitutes the conceptual foundation of the Kavun Adaptive Commercial Leadership Framework (KACL) and the Field Force Operating System (FFOS) introduced throughout this book.

13. FROM FRAMEWORK TO PRACTICE: THE LEADERSHIP TOOLKIT

The preceding chapters explain why adaptive commercial leadership matters. This chapter converts those ideas into a disciplined operating routine. The tools are intentionally lightweight: they are designed to improve the quality, transparency, and learning value of decisions without turning leadership into a bureaucratic exercise.

The central principle is simple: Artificial Intelligence may recommend, forecast, classify, and prioritize, but accountable leaders retain decision rights. Every tool below therefore makes room for evidence, human judgment, ethical challenge, frontline context, and an explicit override path.

13.1 The KACL Readiness Diagnostic

Before selecting technology, leaders should assess whether the organization is ready to use intelligence responsibly. Readiness is not a single score. It is the combined strength of five capabilities: strategic vision, predictive decision intelligence, adaptive organizational learning, human-centered leadership, and ethical governance.

Rate each statement from 1 (not established) to 5 (consistently demonstrated). The purpose is not to produce an attractive average; it is to identify the weakest capability that could undermine the whole operating model.

- Strategic priorities are translated into clear field decisions rather than broad slogans.
- Territory and account decisions use forward-looking indicators as well as historical performance.
- Managers can explain which data and assumptions influence an AI-supported recommendation.
- Frontline feedback is captured, reviewed, and used to improve models and operating routines.
- Coaching conversations integrate performance evidence with individual context and development goals.
- Decision rights are explicit: people know who recommends, who challenges, who approves, and who may override.
- Potential bias, privacy, compliance, and customer-impact risks are reviewed before scale-up.
- Pilots have measurable learning objectives, stopping rules, and accountable owners.
- Leaders reward appropriate challenge instead of treating algorithmic output as unquestionable.
- The organization can trace an important decision from input data through recommendation to human action.

Interpretation: scores below 30 indicate that leadership foundations should be strengthened before a broad deployment. Scores from 30 to 39 support a controlled pilot with strong governance. Scores of 40 or above suggest readiness to scale selectively, provided no single pillar scores materially below the others. These thresholds are managerial prompts, not validated psychometric cutoffs.

13.2 The AI-Supported Decision Canvas

Use this canvas for territory redesign, call-plan prioritization, resource allocation, coaching focus, or another consequential commercial decision. Complete it before approval and revisit it after results are known.

Decision: What choice must be made, by whom, and by what date?

Business objective: Which customer, patient, people, or performance outcome should improve?

Evidence: Which internal and external data are relevant, current, permitted, and sufficiently representative?

AI contribution: Is the system forecasting, ranking, summarizing, detecting anomalies, or generating options?

Assumptions: Which causal beliefs or operating constraints could make the recommendation wrong?

Human context: What does the field team know that may not appear in the data?

Risk review: What could create bias, privacy exposure, regulatory concern, unfair pressure, or loss of trust?

Decision rights: Who recommends, challenges, approves, executes, monitors, and may override?

Success measures: Which leading and lagging indicators will distinguish progress from noise?

Review date: When will the decision be reassessed, and what evidence would trigger reversal?

13.3 A 90-Day Commercial AI Pilot

Days 1–30: Define and de-risk

- Choose one decision problem with a clear owner and a manageable scope.
- Document the current process, baseline performance, known pain points, and compliance boundaries.
- Agree on decision rights, minimum evidence standards, override rules, and stopping conditions.

- Create a cross-functional pilot team that includes commercial leadership, frontline users, analytics, technology, legal, privacy, and compliance as appropriate.

Days 31–60: Test and learn

- Run the AI-supported process alongside the current process before allowing it to influence high-impact decisions.
- Record disagreements between model output and experienced managers; treat those disagreements as learning data.
- Monitor data quality, recommendation stability, adoption friction, unintended incentives, and customer impact.
- Hold a weekly learning review focused on evidence and corrective action rather than project promotion.

Days 61–90: Evaluate and decide

- Compare outcomes with the agreed baseline and examine both performance and decision quality.
- Separate technology limitations from workflow, capability, data, and leadership problems.
- Decide whether to stop, redesign, extend, or scale; record the evidence supporting that decision.
- Translate pilot learning into updated governance controls, training, data requirements, and operating routines.

13.4 The Human-Centered Coaching Protocol

AI-supported coaching should make conversations more specific and fair, not more mechanical. A manager can use the following five-step protocol before and during a coaching discussion.

- Prepare: review relevant evidence, data limitations, recent context, and the employee's stated development goals.
- Ask: invite the employee to interpret the situation before presenting a system-generated conclusion.
- Compare: explore where human observation and analytical signals agree or conflict.
- Choose: agree on one or two observable actions, support requirements, and a review date.
- Learn: evaluate whether the action improved the outcome and whether the analytical recommendation proved useful.

A coaching system should never infer protected characteristics, diagnose a person, or convert opaque scores into irreversible employment decisions. Where employment consequences are possible, qualified human review and applicable legal and organizational safeguards are essential.

13.5 Governance Questions Leaders Must Be Able to Answer

- What decision does the system influence, and how consequential is that decision?
- Who is accountable for the outcome when the recommendation is followed?
- Can the affected manager or employee understand and challenge the recommendation?
- Are the data relevant, lawful, representative, current, and protected?
- How are bias, drift, hallucination, manipulation, and security risks monitored?
- Is there a practical human override, escalation route, and incident-response process?
- What evidence would cause the organization to pause or retire the system?

13.6 Measuring What Matters

Commercial AI should be evaluated as an organizational capability, not merely as a software installation. A balanced scorecard can combine four lenses.

Decision quality: timeliness, forecast accuracy, consistency, reversibility, and the quality of documented assumptions.

Commercial outcomes: appropriate customer coverage, territory opportunity development, execution quality, and sustainable performance.

People and learning: manager coaching quality, adoption, psychological safety, capability growth, and the speed at which lessons alter practice.

Trust and governance: explainability, override use, issue resolution, data quality, fairness indicators, privacy incidents, and compliance findings.

No single metric should dominate. A system that improves a short-term commercial indicator while weakening trust, fairness, compliance, or learning is not a high-performing system.

APPENDIX A. KACL LEADERSHIP REVIEW AGENDA

A monthly 60-minute review keeps the framework operational. The chair should circulate the decision canvas and evidence before the meeting.

- 10 minutes — Strategic context: what changed in the market, portfolio, customer environment, or organization?
- 15 minutes — Decision intelligence: which predictions or recommendations were useful, wrong, unstable, or ignored?
- 10 minutes — Frontline learning: what did managers and representatives observe that the data missed?
- 10 minutes — People leadership: where is coaching, capability, workload, or trust limiting execution?
- 10 minutes — Ethics and governance: which risks, overrides, complaints, or anomalies require action?
- 5 minutes — Commitments: record owners, decisions, review dates, and evidence required for closure.

APPENDIX B. PILOT DECISION RECORD

For each material AI-supported decision, retain a concise record containing the fields below. The record creates traceability without requiring leaders to document every routine judgment.

- Decision identifier, date, accountable owner, and affected business area.
- Decision question and intended outcome.
- Data sources, material exclusions, and known quality limitations.
- System or model used, version where available, and type of output produced.
- Recommendation, confidence or uncertainty information, and key assumptions.
- Human challenge, contextual evidence, and alternative options considered.
- Final decision, rationale, approval, and any override.
- Monitoring measures, review date, observed result, and lessons incorporated.

APPENDIX C. RESPONSIBLE USE COMMITMENT FOR COMMERCIAL LEADERS

A leadership team may adopt the following commitment as a starting point and tailor it to local law, regulation, corporate policy, and risk appetite.

We will use Artificial Intelligence to strengthen evidence-based judgment, organizational learning, and responsible customer engagement. We will not delegate accountability to a model. We will protect privacy, respect regulatory and compliance obligations, examine bias and unintended effects, disclose material limitations to decision makers, maintain meaningful human review, and provide practical routes to question or override recommendations. We will measure success through commercial value, people development, trust, and ethical performance—not efficiency alone.

Limitations

This book presents the **Kavun Adaptive Commercial Leadership Framework (KACL)** as a conceptual leadership model developed from the integration of leadership theory, commercial management literature, Artificial Intelligence research, and the author's professional experience within multinational pharmaceutical organizations.

Several limitations should therefore be acknowledged.

First, the framework is conceptual rather than empirical. Although it is informed by established management literature and practical commercial leadership experience, it has not yet been validated through large-scale quantitative or longitudinal research.

Second, the commercial examples presented throughout this book primarily reflect the pharmaceutical industry. While many of the proposed leadership principles may be applicable to other knowledge-intensive industries, additional research is required before broader generalization can be supported.

Third, Artificial Intelligence technologies continue to evolve rapidly. Consequently, some technological capabilities, implementation practices, and commercial applications described in this book may change as AI systems mature.

Finally, the KACL Framework should be viewed as an evolving leadership model rather than a completed theory. The author welcomes future academic discussion, empirical testing, and constructive refinement that may further strengthen its theoretical and practical contribution.

Future Research

The ideas presented throughout this book represent the beginning of a broader research agenda rather than its conclusion.

Several areas deserve further academic investigation.

Future empirical studies may examine the relationship between AI-supported leadership and commercial performance, evaluate the effectiveness of predictive coaching models, measure the impact of adaptive territory management on organizational outcomes, and assess how Artificial Intelligence influences leadership development within pharmaceutical commercial organizations.

Additional research may also explore the application of the KACL Framework in different healthcare systems, therapeutic areas, organizational structures, and international markets.

Finally, future interdisciplinary collaboration between leadership researchers, commercial executives, healthcare professionals, and Artificial Intelligence specialists may contribute to the continued refinement and empirical validation of adaptive commercial leadership models.

The author hopes that this book encourages further discussion, independent research, and practical experimentation that advance both leadership theory and pharmaceutical commercial excellence.

FINAL AUTHOR'S REFLECTION

"Leadership is not defined by the technology we possess, but by the wisdom with which we choose to use it." — Tevfik Tolga Kavun

Leadership Beyond Artificial Intelligence

When I began my career in pharmaceutical sales more than two decades ago, success was measured primarily through commercial performance.

Sales growth, market share, physician coverage, and business expansion defined professional achievement.

As I gradually assumed broader leadership responsibilities, however, my understanding of success began to change.

I came to realize that organizations do not become exceptional simply because they achieve impressive commercial results.

They become exceptional because they consistently develop people who are capable of creating those results again and again.

Looking back, the most valuable lessons I learned throughout my career rarely emerged from quarterly business reviews or annual performance reports.

They emerged from observing people.

From coaching managers through difficult decisions.

From helping Regional Managers develop future leaders.

From building cross-functional collaboration between commercial, medical, marketing, regulatory, finance, and human resources teams.

From managing uncertainty during periods of organizational growth.

And perhaps most importantly, from recognizing that leadership becomes increasingly important as organizational complexity increases.

Technology continuously changes (Kotter, 2012).

Human leadership remains remarkably constant.

Throughout history, organizations have adopted new products, new software platforms, new communication channels, and new analytical tools.

Each technological generation promised greater efficiency.

Artificial Intelligence represents the most significant transformation of this pattern (Russell & Norvig, 2021).

Unlike previous technological innovations, AI does not simply automate routine activities.

It actively supports managerial thinking.

It analyzes information, identifies hidden patterns, predicts future outcomes, recommends possible actions, and continuously improves its own analytical capability.

This creates extraordinary opportunities for pharmaceutical commercial organizations.

Yet it also creates a new leadership responsibility.

The responsibility is no longer limited to making decisions.

Leaders must now determine how decisions should be made, when Artificial Intelligence should be trusted, when human judgment should prevail, and how organizational values remain protected as technology becomes increasingly influential.

This responsibility cannot be delegated.

It belongs entirely to leadership.

Throughout this book, I have proposed that Artificial Intelligence should be viewed as a leadership multiplier rather than a leadership replacement (Davenport & Harris, 2007).

That belief did not originate from academic theory alone.

It emerged from practical experience accumulated over many years of leading commercial organizations operating in increasingly dynamic environments.

Every organizational transformation reinforced the same conclusion.

Technology improved visibility.

Leadership created direction.

Technology accelerated analysis.

Leadership created trust.

Technology increased efficiency.

Leadership developed people.

Neither capability alone proved sufficient.

Sustainable commercial excellence consistently emerged when both worked together.

This realization ultimately inspired the development of the Kavun Adaptive Commercial Leadership Framework (KACL).

The framework presented throughout this book should not be viewed as a final model.

Rather, it should be considered the beginning of an ongoing conversation about how pharmaceutical commercial leadership may evolve during the coming decades.

Artificial Intelligence will undoubtedly become more capable.

Predictive analytics will become more accurate.

Decision-support systems will become increasingly sophisticated.

Commercial organizations will continue generating larger volumes of information than any individual leader could ever interpret independently.

Despite these developments, I remain convinced that the defining characteristic of outstanding organizations will not be technological sophistication alone.

It will be leadership maturity.

Organizations led by individuals who combine analytical thinking with ethical responsibility, commercial discipline with empathy, and strategic vision with continuous learning will continue to outperform organizations relying solely on technology.

Leadership has never been about possessing all the answers.

Leadership has always been about asking better questions (Senge, 2006).

Artificial Intelligence can help leaders answer questions more quickly.

Only leaders can decide which questions truly matter.

If this book contributes to that conversation—even in a small way—then its purpose has been fulfilled.

My hope is not that readers will simply adopt the ideas presented in these pages.

My hope is that they will challenge them, improve them, adapt them to their own organizations, and continue expanding the conversation around adaptive commercial leadership.

Knowledge advances through dialogue.

Leadership advances through experience.

The future of pharmaceutical commercial excellence will ultimately depend upon both.

Final Leadership Reflection

After more than twenty years in pharmaceutical commercial leadership, one belief has remained unchanged.

Organizations do not achieve sustainable success because they possess the best technology (Barney, 1991).

They achieve sustainable success because they develop leaders capable of using technology wisely, making ethical decisions under uncertainty, and helping other people grow (Heifetz et al., 2009).

Artificial Intelligence will continue to evolve.

Leadership will continue to define how that intelligence is used.

The future therefore belongs not to Artificial Intelligence alone.

It belongs to leaders who understand how to transform intelligence into meaningful human progress.

Closing Quote

"Artificial Intelligence expands what organizations know. Leadership determines what organizations become."

— Tevfik Tolga Kavun

References

Argyris, C., & Schön, D. A. (1978). Organizational learning: A theory of action perspective. Addison-Wesley.

Barney, J. (1991). Firm resources and sustained competitive advantage. Journal of Management, 17(1), 99–120. https://doi.org/10.1177/014920639101700108

Brynjolfsson, E., & McAfee, A. (2014). The second machine age: Work, progress, and prosperity in a time of brilliant technologies. W. W. Norton & Company.

Davenport, T. H., & Harris, J. G. (2007). Competing on analytics: The new science of winning. Harvard Business School Press.

Deloitte. (2024). End-to-end transformation of pharma's commercial activities. https://www.deloitte.com/ie/en/Industries/life-sciences-health-care/research/end-to-end-transformation-of-pharmas-commercial-activities.html

Deloitte. (2025). 2025 life sciences outlook. Deloitte Insights. https://www.deloitte.com/us/en/insights/industry/health-care/life-sciences-and-health-care-industry-outlooks/2025-life-sciences-executive-outlook.html

Drucker, P. F. (2007). Management: Tasks, responsibilities, practices. Transaction Publishers.

Gartner. (2024a, August 12). Accelerate decision making and adaptability to drive commercial growth. https://www.gartner.com/en/documents/5667055

Gartner. (2024b, September 17). Improve learning outcomes and seller performance with adaptive learning. https://www.gartner.com/en/documents/5770115

Gartner. (2024c, September 3). Increase the scale and impact of sales enablement with generative AI. https://www.gartner.com/en/documents/5731183

Gartner. (2025). What good leadership looks like in an AI world. https://www.gartner.com/en/articles/the-future-of-leadership-with-ai

Goleman, D., Boyatzis, R. E., & McKee, A. (2013). Primal leadership: Unleashing the power of emotional intelligence. Harvard Business Review Press.

Heifetz, R. A., Grashow, A., & Linsky, M. (2009). The practice of adaptive leadership: Tools and tactics for changing your organization and the world. Harvard Business Press.

IQVIA. (2024). Gen AI: The next frontier of life sciences commercial excellence. https://www.iqvia.com/events/2024/03/gen-ai-the-next-frontier-of-life-sciences-commercial-excellence

Kahneman, D. (2011). Thinking, fast and slow. Farrar, Straus and Giroux.

Kotter, J. P. (2012). Leading change. Harvard Business Review Press.

McKinsey & Company. (2024a). Early adoption of generative AI in commercial life sciences. https://www.mckinsey.com/industries/life-sciences/our-insights/early-adoption-of-generative-ai-in-commercial-life-sciences

McKinsey & Company. (2024b). Generative AI in the pharmaceutical industry: Moving from hype to reality. https://www.mckinsey.com/industries/life-sciences/our-insights/generative-ai-in-the-pharmaceutical-industry-moving-from-hype-to-reality

McKinsey & Company. (2025a). Scaling gen AI in the life sciences industry. https://www.mckinsey.com/industries/life-sciences/our-insights/scaling-gen-ai-in-the-life-sciences-industry

McKinsey & Company. (2025b). Simplification for success: Rewiring the biopharma operating model. https://www.mckinsey.com/industries/life-sciences/our-insights/simplification-for-success-rewiring-the-biopharma-operating-model

McKinsey & Company. (2025c). Reimagining life science enterprises with agentic AI. https://www.mckinsey.com/industries/life-sciences/our-insights/reimagining-life-science-enterprises-with-agentic-ai

McKinsey & Company. (2026). The future of B2B sales: How growth champions rewire their playbooks with AI. https://www.mckinsey.com/capabilities/growth-marketing-and-sales/our-insights/the-future-of-b2b-sales-how-growth-champions-rewire-their-playbooks-with-ai

Mintzberg, H. (1973). The nature of managerial work. Harper & Row.

Mökander, J., Sheth, M., Gersbro-Sundler, M., Blomgren, P., & Floridi, L. (2024). Challenges and best practices in corporate AI governance: Lessons from the biopharmaceutical industry. arXiv. https://arxiv.org/abs/2407.05339

Nonaka, I., & Takeuchi, H. (1995). The knowledge-creating company: How Japanese companies create the dynamics of innovation. Oxford University Press.

OECD. (2024). OECD AI principles. https://www.oecd.org/en/topics/ai-principles.html

Payne, A., & Frow, P. (2005). A strategic framework for customer relationship management. Journal of Marketing, 69(4), 167–176. https://doi.org/10.1509/jmkg.2005.69.4.167

Piercy, N. F., & Lane, N. (2009). Strategic customer management: Strategizing the sales organization. Oxford University Press.

Porter, M. E. (1985). Competitive advantage: Creating and sustaining superior performance. Free Press.

Porter, M. E., & Teisberg, E. O. (2006). Redefining health care: Creating value-based competition on results. Harvard Business School Press.

Russell, S. J., & Norvig, P. (2021). Artificial intelligence: A modern approach (4th ed.). Pearson.

Senge, P. M. (2006). The fifth discipline: The art & practice of the learning organization (Rev. ed.). Currency.

Sinha, P., Shastri, A., & Lorimer, S. (2024, September 3). Can AI assistants add value to your sales team? Harvard Business Review. https://hbr.org/2024/09/can-ai-assistants-add-value-to-your-sales-team

Taleb, N. N. (2007). The black swan: The impact of the highly improbable. Random House.

World Health Organization. (2021). Ethics and governance of artificial intelligence for health: WHO guidance. https://www.who.int/publications/i/item/9789240029200

Zoltners, A. A., Sinha, P., & Lorimer, S. E. (2009). Building a winning sales force: Powerful strategies for driving high performance. AMACOM.

www.ingramcontent.com/pod-product-compliance
Lightning Source LLC
LaVergne TN
LVHW060548061126
851857LV00017B/1935